North Shields The Bombing of a Town

by Ron Curran

In Honour of all who fought

The Service Men and Women and Civilians

1939-1945

Copyright Ron Curran 2009

First published in 2009 by

Summerhill Books
PO Box 1210
Newcastle-upon-Tyne
NE99 4AH

Email: andrew_clark@hotmail.co.uk

ISBN: 978-1-906721-21-3

Printed by: CVN Print, Maxwell Street, South Shields

Contents

Abbreviations

Please note abbreviations relating to bombing are thus:

HEs   High Explosive Bombs

IBs   Incendiary Bombs (small bombs with fins that fell in their hundreds)

OBs   Oil Bombs that threw burning oil over wide area of damage

LM   Land Mines had huge explosive power

PM   Mine dropped by parachute that exploded at ground level causing great surface damage

UXB   Unexploded Bomb

Other common abbreviations include:

AFS   Auxiliary Fire Service

ARP   Air Raid Precautions

ATS   Auxiliary Territorial Service – Women's army during the war

LDV   Local Defence Volunteers – later to become the Home Guard (Dad's Army)

WAAF   Women's Auxiliary Air Force

WLA   Women's Land Army

WRENS   Women's Royal Naval Service

WVS   Women's Voluntary Service

A famous wartime message – 'Careless Talk Costs Lives'. This campaign warned people not to talk about the war in case spies were listening and would report back to Germany.

4

Introduction

I believe that the most significant thing that ever happened to North Shields must have been the bombing of the town in the Second World War. That is not to say that other nearby towns did not equally suffer, although communications being what they were in those war time days, we were not to know until much later. But rumours travel quickly and even after the terrible bombing of Hull, it was known about on the streets of North Shields within a couple of days. It was much later, however, before it was confirmed. Likewise, I was only able to confirm the number of dead and injured at Wilkinson's shelter some time after the war. But we knew it was very serious. North Shields suffered some very serious bombing, mainly on civilian homes. An excellent account of this time can be found in a book called *The Most Dangerous Enemy – a History of the Battle of Britain* by Stephen Bungay (2001), possibly the most definitive record of the bombing of Britain yet written, drawing upon not only British records but also German records of the Battle of Britain. I have also drawn upon *North East Diary, 1939-1945* by Roy Ripley and Brian Pears which gives a meticulous account of air raids upon the North East of England and the consequences. Better than that however is to be able to draw upon my own memories of that time. However, because of the book and diary described above, I am now able to give dates – and even times to most of the events that I will relate in this book. These were the most significant days of my life as, from the first day when war was declared to the last when the war ended, life was a lottery and odds were shortened considerably during air raids. I consider myself very lucky.

As you will appreciate, 1939 when the war started is now 70 years ago (at the time of writing) and it ended 64 years ago so it is a drag on anybody's memory to factually remember the dates of these events even if the events themselves will never fade. However, because I want to keep the thread of the whole story in perspective, I believe that the dates are necessary. I have therefore inserted my memories within the specific time line. As I reflect on the war years, other memories, once forgotten, spring to mind. Six years is a long time in a young person's life, and from twelve years old to eighteen years old are probably the most formative years of anybody's life. They are normally the years when boys and girls are growing from adolescence to adults and living in hope, looking towards the future. But during these dark years there were restrictions in everything – in travel, communications, food, recreation, employment and even education. I hope I can draw an adequate picture that will ring bells with anybody old enough to remember the war, but also open the eyes of those who were lucky enough to miss it.

This is primarily a story about the bombing of North Shields during the war, not a story about myself. However, I would hope you will allow me to be the vehicle of transcription, allowing me to give a very local account wherever possible, in other words, seeing the war in North Shields through my own eyes. Our town was very badly bombed and I want the present inhabitants and others to know that. As far as I am aware, no one has ever yet written the story of North Shields in those years and it deserves to be told. Many people died and many more were injured, some very seriously. And some were heroes and heroines in many ways. Some were honoured and unfortunately some were not. The legacy of that is bound to be remembered. But of one thing I am certain, the spirit of the people of the area, their warmth and character came out in greater focus then, when it was sorely needed as never before.

Ron Curran
2009

Chapter 1
North Shields Before The War

I was born in 1927 and lived in what was surely the centre of North Shields at the time and probably still is. This was in Church Way at number 57, where the Sir James Knott Youth Centre (now YMCA) stands and its front door is as near as can be guessed where our entrance up a stone passage was. Just up the street was the parish church of Christ Church, notable at that time for its bell ringing. Every Sunday the bells chimed and everyone wore their Sunday best and almost all children attended Sunday School. The men donned their white scarves (only on a Sunday), best flat cap and often a carnation in their lapel. The women were making the

Sunday dinner, or struggling to find something to make it with. These were the really hard up days when the town's very own Boot and Shoe fund was established by a former mayor of the town, Alderman Isaac Black, a well known businessman in the area. The boots and shoes were distributed through the schools to those in need of footwear and my mother forbade us to put our names down, even if our shoes leaked on a rainy day. She would repair them with her cast iron 'last', pieces of leather, nails and a small hammer. My dad, she said, was useless with a hammer.

Also in our street, up past Christ Church and where Preston Hospital was situated, was the town Work House. As kids, we used to watch the men trudge down the street looking in the gutters for cigarette ends and, when finding them, stuff the remnants of the tobacco into a tin box. At another time you would see them rolling cigarettes with this filth. I was horrified.

A North Shields lane in the 1930s.

A busy river scene at North Shields with HMS Queen Mary in the foreground.

Sir James Knott Memorial Flats – A well known North Shields landmark.

At the bottom of the street was a Soup Kitchen which I understand was established for the General Strike in 1926, a year before I was born, but still used when I was a child. I remember a lady with a little boy passing down the street, who apparently knew me. She spoke my name and asked if I would like a bowl of soup and I am sure I must have said yes. She then took me to the Soup Kitchen. When my mother asked where I had been she 'went mad'. 'Don't ever go there again' she said. I didn't know why she said that but can guess it was her independence speaking. There was also a communal wash house in our street (by the way, these were large Victorian style buildings) and again my mother would not use it, preferring to exercise her biceps on the communal mangle in the backyard.

Celebrations in North Shields – Empire Day.

My memory of Easter Sundays was of all the churches in the town marching the children with their own Sunday School banner and led by the Salvation Army to Northumberland Square which was just around the corner from where I lived. The mayor and church dignitaries presided and we sang hymns and listened to sermons and after it was over we were marched back to our church, St Andrew's, which was in Camden Street and was only just off Northumberland Square itself. When we arrived we were all given a small present of perhaps an apple or orange, listened to a short sermon from our own Sunday School Superintendent and then dispersed. We did the same at Harvest Festival. However, the time I remember best was the Silver Jubilee of King George V and Queen Mary when the whole of Northumberland Square was flagged and garlanded and all the children of all the schools in the borough were marched as before to be addressed by the mayor and other dignitaries. We were all given a mug and two medals. This was an ornate mug with the faces of the King and Queen embossed upon it, and beautiful large silver medals. If I had them now I could claim quite a sum on any of the antique road shows that now prevail on the television. Not forgetting that the mugs were stuffed with candies.

I also watched the RSM *Olympic* sail into the Tyne in 1935 to be scrapped at Hebburn, and I remember the first traffic lights erected at the top of our street where Ye Olde Hundred pub now stands on one side of Church Way and the Queen's Head on the other. Also the introduction of Belisha Beacons, those flashing orange globes at crossing places that later became better known as Zebra Crossings. The Belisha Beacons were introduced in about 1934 and all the school children received Belisha Beacon lollipops. The name comes from the Home Secretary of the day, Mr Hoare Belisha who introduced this scheme. Although I was aware that these were hard times, I also sensed that it was a sublime period when the sun seemed to shine more often, when it was quieter with much less traffic and no blaring 'music'. A time when respect for others was a built in requirement for children. We were told, 'Children are to be seen and not heard.'

They are now far off days, and too much water has passed under the bridge to know the reason for such a change. But then again, this can also have been said by our own parents and grandparents about the Industrial Revolution. We might complain about those days or, on the other hand, wish that some of them were back. But you can't have it both ways. I left Church Way in 1935-36 in a glorious summer. We were taken in an ambulance (it had darkened windows) to Moor Park Hospital where our clothes, furniture and bed linen was taken to be fumigated to ensure that none of the bugs/germs or whatever were carried to our new house in the new Ridges Estate at No 57, Laburnum Avenue. We were then taken to a green wooden hut on the Coast Road where we stayed overnight. This hut later became a weighing machine hut for the council, in which Graham Sylph, an artist friend of mine, worked after the war. It was at this hut that my dad came from work to meet us. How we got home I cannot remember.

Fish Quay, North Shields. 455

More memories of the old town – A postcard view of North Shields Fish Quay.

I refute emphatically that the Ridges Estate was an estate of difficult tenants, either in the way they lived or their financial commitments. I became a councillor for Percy Ward which covered a sizeable part of the estate and can perhaps as well as anyone else or, even better, speak on their behalf. First they were multi-cultural, moral and honest. They were also tough, as they had to be to survive the rigours of poverty. They were more often than not also scrupulously clean. That there would have been a small number who let those standards down I don't doubt, but never to the extent that they needed to change the name of every street, the name of the estate, and even the name of the local pub, the Ridges Inn. This was a stigma visited upon the people of the Ridges which was only refuted by the valour of so many of those families whose sons and daughters fought and died for us in the last war. I knew many of them personally, as air raid wardens, a Red Beret in the Parachute Regiment (who became a champion heavyweight boxer), merchant seamen and soldiers.

An aerial view of the Ridges Estate.

As the war grew closer, even children could feel the tension in the air, from the conversations in the home, talk overheard from neighbours, and even references by teachers, some of whom were being called up (conscripted). Hitler's name became predominant, until with us kids he became the proverbial bogey man. History and geography lessons seem to be adapted to the changing times, as Hitler entered Austria in 1938 and attacked Poland in 1939. Although not all the kids were as interested as I was, perhaps it was just as well insofar the less interested they were, the less frightened they were. Our home however had been a political house as long as I can remember. We of course were Labour and our colours at that time were black and yellow. Our parents had followed the Spanish Civil War in 1936 to the invasion of Finland by Russia in 1939.

Chapter 2
The Day War Broke Out

I was twelve years old when war was declared on 3rd September 1939. I remember this as a warm, sunny day and was playing in the street when a window opened above and someone shouted, 'We are at war, we are at war'. The neighbours turned up their radio and the whole street fell silent. I did not know at the time but it was the voice of Mr Neville Chamberlain the then prime minister saying that we had declared war on Germany. Almost within minutes the air raid siren wailed – the most horrible banshee wailing I have ever heard apart from the German Stuka dive bombers that came later. My mother ran out of the house and ushered us in under the stairs. I am sure it was a Sunday. By the way, it wasn't everyone who had a 'wireless' in those days – it was regarded as a luxury. After about what seemed like twenty minutes, the all clear siren went and we all trooped out from under the stairs and went into the street to share the excitement with other kids, although not a thing had happened apart from the air raid sirens howling. By the way, I think my dad was having his Sunday pint down at the local in Shields, as we termed the town centre. As a veteran of both the Boer War and the First World War, we felt safe when he was around.

I should at this point say that our family was pretty political insofar that events such as the Spanish Civil War and the Russian invasion of Finland were discussed between my father and mother. I also had to go to a local house in Marina Avenue to pick up the *Daily Worker*, that I later found was a newspaper of the British Communist Party. Because I knew that we supported Labour I asked my mother who the communists were. She said 'Ask your dad'. I had heard him arguing one day with his brother Patrick before the war started, who was visiting us from Edinburgh. It was a heated conversation about the Russians 'not helping Spain', which I found later meant not supporting the International Brigade who were fighting in Spain to support the

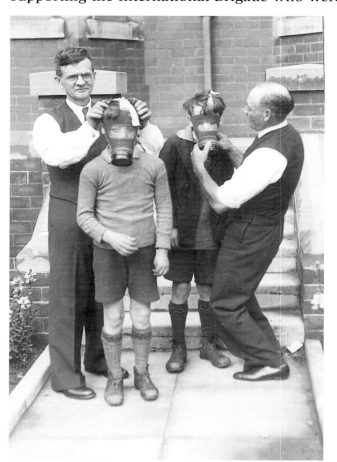

North East children trying their gas masks in 1939.

democratically elected government. When I eventually asked my dad who the communists were, he said bluntly, 'Not much better than the bloody Germans'.

'Why do you buy the *Daily Worker* then?' I asked.

'Because I like to read about the other side' he replied.

It was a simple answer and sounded good enough to me. In November 1939, two months after the war started the Russians invaded Finland and my dad was very angry. Again I heard him arguing, this time with Patrick's son, also called Patrick (who was a grown up) who lived in Wallsend although, like my dad, born in Scotland. I suspected Patrick was a communist like his dad. However, I do know that he became a Labour supporter after the Finland incident.

As children we already knew our neighbours (not a common thing nowadays) and respected their authority. They would advise us to get to the shelters if the sirens had sounded or if the barrage balloons had started to rise high into the sky, a fairly sure sign of an approaching raid. We became fairly knowledgeable of approaching air raids at night time. First the searchlights

The front page of the Daily Express announces the rationing that will come into force in the first months of the war in 1939. The newspaper also features the battle Finland was having with the Soviet Union.

would go on one after another and the barrage balloons could be seen rising higher into the sky. These huge monsters looked like silver elephants and trailed tails of about two dozen wires about fifteen foot long which presumably was to cut or damage any aeroplane unfortunate enough to encounter them. Anyway, it seemed to give us a safety umbrella and kept the German planes high enough to prevent accurate bombing. At least that's what we kids thought. The last and most obvious sign of an impending night air raid was what I would call the 'signal' searchlight, which always swept the sky in circles for what seemed like a few minutes and always before a bombing raid.

The Years of Fear

This was to be a period of apprehension for all of us, as it was a cloud that pervaded every waking moment of the day and night. Horror stories of German atrocities abroad gave us little confidence for the future. I remember my mother saying that some of the first internees in Germany were active trade unionists, which immediately caused us concern about father who was a union official at the local pit in Wallsend, the Rising Sun Colliery. But my parents put on a brave face, especially dad, who as a veteran soldier had actually looked death in the face more than once. As an army veteran of both the Boer War and the Great War, we felt some degree of safety when he was with us. He joined what was then called the LDV, the Local Defence Volunteers, which was the forerunner of the proverbial Dad's Army of the TV series – The Home Guard.

That first day is remembered by all who lived during that time. Almost immediately after the announcement by Neville Chamberlain that war on Germany had been declared, the air raid sirens wailed their unearthly banshee sound and everybody put on their gas masks, scattered indoors, under the stairs if they had any, or wherever there was some sort of shelter. The air raid shelters had not yet been built of course. It was only in the course of time that we got to know that the air raid sirens had sounded throughout Britain at precisely the same time. Only recently in Scotland at my art class we were reminiscing about that day, and we all said the same thing. So it was a test, wasn't it? A chance to test the air raid sirens and the nerve of the people at the same time.

It was in late 1940 when the first real test arrived, with some sporadic raids on Tyneside. A number of daylight and night time raids brought home the reality of war, when we first heard of deaths in the town. During this early period of the war there was great activity among the civil defence, with air raid wardens being issued with steel helmets and whistles, and woe betide anyone who showed a chink of light through their curtains. The shout of "Put those lights out" by the warden would be taken up by everyone else until it became a familiar phrase during the war. The blackout was something that has to be experienced to believe. A total blackout and yet people were walking about their business and even recognising neighbours as their eyes became more accustomed to the darkness. On a moonlight night, the silvery beams lit up the streets and it was like manna from heaven, but it was on these nights that we could expect air raids, when the River Tyne would be lit up like a silver road map beckoning the enemy to its target. We would then see the barrage balloons rise high into the sky and the searchlights switch on and we knew that a raid was due.

In areas of the town where open space allowed, large RAF vehicles manned by WAAFs (Women's Auxiliary Air Force) with an RAF corporal in charge were busy inflating the huge barrage balloons that soon became a permanent feature over the period of the war. These enormous flying elephants were to play a large part in making the observant population aware that an air raid was imminent, when they simultaneously rose into the air, scores of them, above busy Tyneside. It would not be long before the thrum-thrum-thrum drone that was unique to the German bombers

An artist's impression of the River Tyne on a moonlight night during the last war. This is an imaginative painting, from memory as I believed it would appear. I have shown a peep at the South Shields Ferry Landing as I remember it. By Ron Curran in 2005.

The light beams out into the night sky in search of enemy aircraft. Planes caught in the searchlight would soon be the target of ant-aircraft guns.

alone, could be heard. And then the anti-aircraft artillery would burst out in a roar that was louder than any bomb that I ever heard go off. During a raid at night, one only had to look out of the Anderson air raid shelter built into the garden, to see "flaming onions" soaring into the sky, orange tracer shells that guided the gunners to their target, then the deafening roar of a burst of anti-aircraft guns, and then the flares dropped by enemy planes that seemed to light up the whole sky. If it wasn't so dangerous it could be likened to a huge firework display. And then the shrapnel from our own guns would rain down. It wasn't healthy to be outside. Of course, the drama was heightened by the searchlights which at intervals lit up the barrage balloons hanging like silver elephants in the dark night sky. Another pointer to an imminent air-raid at night was the 'sentinel' searchlight which stood rigid and upright and then would begin a circling movement in the sky. Immediately, scores of searchlights up and down the Tyne stabbed out into the darkness.

On two particular occasions, during a storm, lightning struck quite a number of the barrage balloons which then burst into flames and slowly descended as red and yellow sheets of flammable material and landed in a shower of sparks over their particular town. On one single occasion I counted eleven balloons that suffered this fate. These were spectacular sights to see. To the uninitiated who may wonder about the use of these floating monsters, it would be helpful to say that they had an array of thin steel cables attached to their underside which hung down about twenty feet or more and created quite a hazard to flying aircraft. Imagine scores of these things floating at several-thousand feet in the air. It kept enemy aircraft at a higher level than was necessary for good bomb aiming. Another and greater deterrent to the enemy aircraft were the fighter planes, Spitfires and Hurricanes which were regularly seen over our town. On a number of occasions we saw dog-fights high in the sky.

It wasn't long before the bombing that we saw the first instances of being at war when lorries arrived in the street to unload the galvanized air raid shelters for those lucky enough to have back gardens (or front gardens). These were then dug about three feet into the ground and covered with a layer of earth at least a foot deep. I always thought they were safe. Certainly better than under the stairs, as it wasn't long before we found out, not at our house, mind you. Another innovation was the

Children crowd around while the metal sheets for the Anderson Shelters are unloaded from a lorry at the beginning of the war. The shelters were soon to become a common sight throughout Britain.

introduction of gas masks, which we all had to wear, or so we thought, whenever their was an air raid. They were kept in square cardboard boxes which were held around our necks with string and we had to take them to school and back every day. Putting them on was a claustrophobic experience. I can only remember that we ceased wearing them after a few air raids and no gas attacks ensued.

We went down to the river a lot during the war. Ships sailed into the River Tyne escorted by minesweepers, which appeared to be converted trawlers trailing what I believe were called 'paravanes' behind them on long lines of thin steel hawser. They trailed on either side of the sweeper and were credited with cutting the length of steel rope that held the mine just under the surface. The paravanes were hollow tubes with fins like torpedoes, and watching these minesweepers always reminded you of the dangers of the sea. Many merchant seamen from Tyneside died during the war, particularly from South Shields which had a large percentage of the Tyneside seamen. But North Shields also had its fair share and many were the neighbours who lived near us who suffered the grief of a lost husband, father or son. In 1941, the air raids increased and between April and October of that year there were a number of very heavy raids on North Shields. Two of these, on a Tuesday and Thursday of the same week were dive-bombing raids by German Stuka aircraft. The terrifying scream of the aircraft, which dived steeply to drop their bombs, was produced by special sirens attached to their wings. It was like the howling of a hundred banshees, then would come the shriek of the bomb, with a much shorter life but with terrifying consequences. We used to crouch in the air raid shelter not knowing whether it was our turn next.

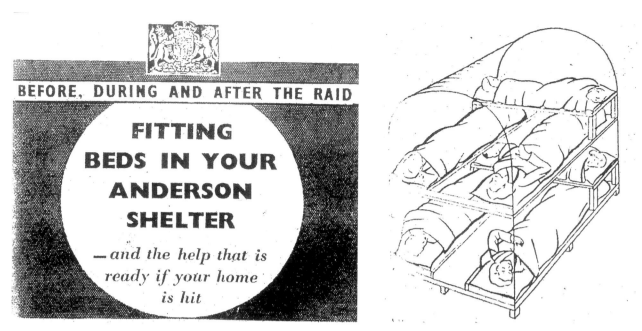

A leaflet was issued by the Ministry of Home Security advising people how to fit bunk beds in their Anderson Shelter. The illustration on the right shows the bunk beds that were 6 ft 6 ins long and 20 inches wide for the adults and 4 foot 6 ins long and 2 feet wide for the children.

This Anderson Shelter is nearing completion with soil covering the metal structure. The shelters were named after Sir John Anderson who was responsible for preparing air raid precautions.

A Lucky Escape

On a number of nights incendiary bombs rained down and the area was lit up in a ghastly green light. I remember a lot of heroic people those nights climbing on to roofs of buildings to dislodge the burning phosphorous. The raids were heavy and indiscriminate, or the Germans were bad shots? All around our street in Laburnum Avenue, bombs fell near the vicinity of our house, Maple Crescent, Silky's Lane, Blackthorn Crescent, The Quadrant, houses behind the Pineapple Inn, the Rex Cinema, and Waterville Road, each of them not being more than, at the furthest, quarter of a mile. Of course there were many more fell elsewhere in the town. The worst incident was on May 3rd 1941 when a single bomb fell onto Wilkinson's lemonade factory, where underneath was an air raid shelter. The bomb fell through the roof and demolished the entire factory including the huge water tank, and landed in the air raid shelter. Official records say over 100 people died. It was one of the worst bombing incidents in Britain. My mother had a lucky escape that very night. She and a neighbour called Mrs Sweeting worked at Tyne Brand down by the Fish Quay and nicknamed The Tin Factory. On their way home when the sirens sounded, they would normally rush for this shelter under Wilkinson's lemonade factory. My mother used to say that it was so cheerful with so many civilians, sailors and other servicemen, one of whom played an accordion. On the night it got hit, my mother and her friend had passèd this shelter by several streets and decided, rather than go back, to try and get home 'for the sake of the kids'. How lucky they were.

The Army Cadets

There were uniforms everywhere during the war, worn by both men and women. The Home Guard, Air Raid Wardens, Soldiers, Sailors and Airmen, ATS, WRENS and WAAFs each one respectively the women's branch of the former. Not to forget of course, the Land Army girls and their uniforms. Not to be outdone, I had joined the Army Cadets and I attended the Annual Cadet Camp at Ponteland (shown in picture below) which consisted of rows of wooden huts, and I had a whale of a time as battalion bugler. While at the camp we visited the rifle range. I quite liked the idea of practising but not shooting anyone in real life. As I was aiming to take a pot shot, an officer cautioned me about how I was aiming. "Why are you holding your rifle on a skew?" he asked. I knew what he meant. I could not focus with my right eye, only with my left, which for a right hander was 'skew handed'. I told him about my right eye which I found out later according to the optician, was what he called a bent reflex, caused he believed by the measles. The officer called me off the range and said I couldn't shoot there, and that he would report this to my captain. That was the first time I had noticed a deficiency in my right eye. Some years later, just prior to being

Ron Curran (author) third from the right standing with rifle and bugle on his right shoulder. A number of names still remain in my memory. (Roy) Richardson as I always knew him at school is now Sergeant Major sitting behind the white shirted lad at the front; Ron Stronach, the corporal standing third from the left; Jimmie Craig, who became a policeman, second from left right at the back. The lad next to me on my right (your left) had my same birthday on the same day, month and year (1927) but I forget his name. The captain seated in the middle front with the football was celebrating a broken foot. The most senior officer, the Major, is seated immediately to the captain's left (your right).

elected onto the council, I had an eye test at an opticians shop in Bedford Street. He told me I had a bent reflex and the he thought it may have been caused by measles. Had I had measles he asked. I said yes. He then said something very surprising. "May I advise you to see your doctor to have a hearing test. I am sure that your hearing will have been affected" – which I did. I was then sent to Preston Hospital where a specialist in a white gown told me soberly, "I am sorry to have to tell you that your hearing in your right ear is badly impaired and will get progressively worse. You have nerve deafness." Bang therefore goes an army career. I really wasn't worried but if I were a parent now with young children I would take measles very seriously indeed.

The 'Invasion' of Tyneside

One of my most hair-raising experiences in the cadets was the 'invasion' of Tyneside by a number of Scottish regiments, to test the defences of the Home Guard in the North Tyneside area. We had been warned beforehand to expect them within the next twelve hours (so I was told by the older Home Guard members). Our platoon had to man the North Shields Gasworks at Minton Lane, which was about a mile from where I lived. We established ourselves in the clocking-in office at the entrance and I was given the job as a messenger. We were of course all in army uniform and I remember being quite a big lad for seventeen years old. I ran a couple of messages before darkness, but as soon as darkness fell the gates were closed and we were ensconced in this brick cabin. I cannot quite remember how they passed the time but I do know I was let out through a side door a number of times "to see what is happening" as they put it. To let you know the layout, Minton Road (which we locally called Gasworks Road) had a high wall running the full length of the gasworks. On the other side of the road running parallel, was a large fenced-in area of allotments, all with footpaths which led out into 'Gasworks Road'.

This was an ideal situation for an ambush on our post. In the darkness these entrances looked forbidding and I would glance out over to the allotments, up and down the street and pop back and say "Its ok". I couldn't have seen a Scottish soldier any more than I could have seen a chimney sweep on that dark night. What I did wonder about was why there were no sentries posted outside. But I was just a boy, it wasn't for me to question why. I may not have liked the answer! Dawn broke, and still no invasion so I was asked to do another "look see". Again I stepped outside and still saw nothing. Suddenly, a banshee-wailing split the air and simply scores of kilted

Home Guardsmen, probably from 7th Northumberland (Tynemouth) Battalion, at Cullercoats.

Home Guardsmen of the Signals Section of 7th Northumberland (Tynemouth) Battalion.

soldiers ran out of their hiding places in the allotments. It must have been a literal rabbit warren of 'foreign' bodies who, in the lifting darkness and under the lightening-sky, raced out into the road. I had a head start, already being outside, and hared down the road to the frenzy of screams from these hideous invaders. They had levelled their guns that crackled with gunfire caused by pulling a cord which exploded realistic crackers.

But worse than that was when they threw clay hand grenades which exploded at my feet. Had I been on the front line I would have died a thousand deaths, but as it was I lived to run the full length of the road, right down to the closed dock gates and I leapt for the top. However, I was dragged down and told I was dead and a yellow chalk mark was made on my uniform. I have no idea what happened to the rest of the platoon. I never saw them again. But I know one thing, if it had been the Germans we never stood a chance. My father also came home several hours after me wearing a yellow chalk mark. But his entrance caused a scare which we would never forget. He must have tiptoed up the passage and entered the living room holding a gun at us and shouting "hands up". My mother shrieked and recognising him shouted, "You silly fool, put that gun down and don't ever do that again". He then told us that North Tyneside had been successfully invaded "by the Jocks" and that he had been cornered and 'shot'. He was officially dead. So was I.

Some months later I was persuaded to take up boxing by the Captain of the Cadet Company. During one of our work-outs at the Hawkey's Lane Boys Club he told me that a visiting senior officer, who had inspected our company in the Spring Gardens School yard some time before, had recommended me for promotion to officer rank. What did I think? I left the cadets immediately and for good. I could see that this 'promotion' might lead me into an army career, and that was the last thing I wanted. Although at this time I didn't know what I wanted as a career, it wasn't to kill people. That was the end of my 'army life' and I left the cadets shortly afterwards.

Rationing

Apart from the black-out, that dampener of social life (although, how could you complain when soldiers, sailors and airmen were fighting?), there was food rationing, where coupons were provided for sugar, butter, eggs, meat, chocolate, sweets and cigarettes and even silk stockings etc. The shortage of food gave lessons to housewives on prudence and inventiveness. Dried milk, dried eggs and dried potatoes became part of the staple diet. The young women of the day painted their legs a horrible orange brown and drew a black line down the back. Somebody with a flair for art could have made a mint painting their legs?

Talking of that, a black market grew and prospered from the shortages, and I have no doubt that the 'barrow boys' of civvie street were as clever as the sharp lads in the army who would never pass through a farmyard on exercise without coming out the other end with a tin helmet full of eggs and a chicken in his gas mask holder. Anyone who has seen the film *All Quiet on the Western Front* will know what I mean. We used to receive food hampers from my mother's two sisters in London, my Aunt Edith and Aunt Dorothy. They were both 'in service' even though well into their fifties, being 'war spinsters' of the First World War. If I can just divert for a moment to explain. During the Great War, so many young men never returned to their sweethearts due to the enormous loss of young lives on the Western Front, leaving behind thousands of young women, many of whom never married. There were so many women and so few men. My mother's family was a family of two boys and five girls. Of the five girls, three never married. Years later my mother asked me to take her on a car run to Stanhope in County Durham. When we arrived there she asked me to stop at the war memorial for the First World War. She then pointed out the name of Oliver Bainbridge, my Aunt Jennie's sweetheart who was killed in France. Then she pointed across the road to the Pack Horse Inn and told me that an aunt of hers ran it many years ago and both my mother and her sister Janet worked there during the First World War. (I have since verified this on the 1911 Census Returns.) The visit must have held sad memories. She then told me that sisters Edith and Dorothy had both lost their boyfriends also. These two aunties were having a hell of a time in the London Blitz. What we experienced was nothing in comparison, although they do say of course, that if a bomb falls down a chimney while you are raking the fireplace, your number must be on it.

The spice of life is very much Clara Carrot's concern; for she's a master of variety — a quick-change artist with a hundred and one disguises, each more amusing than the last. If you've only met her plain and boiled you've no idea how delightful she can be in other modes. You should try

Jugged Brisket

1½ lbs. brisket, 2 lbs. carrots, 2 tablespoons dripping, 1½ pts. vegetable stock, 1 tablespoon gravy thickening, 2 tablespoons piquant sauce or vinegar from pickle bottle, 1 saltspoon mustard. Melt the dripping in a stout saucepan. Grate half the carrot into it. Put in the meat, then the rest of the grated carrot. Pour in 1 pint stock. Cover saucepan, simmer 2 hrs. Thicken rest of stock with gravy thickening. Add sauce and mustard, pour into pot and cook fast for 10 mins. A grand dish, to serve 4 or 5.

With food shortages people were encouraged to eat more carrots.

A doodle bug falls from the sky over the south of England.

They told us about the doodle bugs, those nasty rockets called respectively, the V1 and V2. They were fired in France and travelled over the English Channel and over the coast to London. Aeroplanes tried to intercept them over the sea and tip over their wings. The drone of these rockets ceased suddenly and then plunged to the earth. You can imagine the terror of the inhabitants below if the noise suddenly ceased above their heads. These aunts visited us on a number of occasions and when I look back, I can only salute them for their courage and thank them for their food parcels. They must have known that my mother was having a hard time economically.

Spitfire Fund

In the summer of 1940 – when the Battle of Britain was at its height – the Mayor of the Borough of Tynemouth launched at Spitfire Fund. On the right is his letter starting the campaign to raise £5,000 to 'purchase a Spitfire Fighter'.

The *Morning News*, 29th August 1940 reported:

'The Major of Tynemouth (Ald R.T. Smith) is determined to have a Spitfire in a month and a further appeal is made to the people of the borough in the new window advertisement to be displayed shortly in the windows of the North Shields Electricity Department.

'Mr J.D. Bolton, chief assistant at the Borough Treasurer's office is making a five-foot poster of a man striking a blow with a hammer to ring the bell at the top of a scale. The man represents you, the people of this town, and the bell is the £5,000 for the Spitfire.'

MAYOR'S PARLOUR,
TOWN HALL,
TYNEMOUTH.

Dear Sir, Madam,

BOROUGH OF TYNEMOUTH "SPITFIRE" FUND.

As a result of many requests, I have inaugurated an appeal to the inhabitants of the Borough for the sum of £5,000 to purchase a " Spitfire " Fighter for the Royal Air Force. I hope to raise this amount within one month.

The Battle of Britain is now on, and as the Premier said in his speech in the House of Commons on Tuesday last, "The gratitude of every home in our island, in our Empire and indeed, throughout the world, goes out to the British airmen who, undaunted by odds, unwearied in their constant challenge and mortal danger, are turning the tide of world war by their prowess and by their devotion. Never in the field of human conflict was so much owed by so many to so few."

Our airmen are magnificent, we owe a huge debt to them all and in particular to our Fighter Pilots.

In a recent mass raid on the North East Coast our Fighter Pilots gave a splendid account of themselves, inflicting severe losses on the enemy.

We are fighting to preserve the safety of this country of which we are all so justly proud, we are also fighting for the dignity, freedom and the rights of man and a better world. We are driving our way to peace and victory over Nazi tyranny ; and I make this personal appeal to you to assist in bringing the day of glorious victory nearer with a speedy return to peace, by giving generously to the Borough of Tynemouth " Spitfire " Fund.

The fund is for a very great cause—may I add perhaps the greatest for which a fund has ever been inaugurated. Every subscription received, however small the amount, is a blow at the enemy—a blow in the great battle for freedom and peace.

Your donation may be forwarded to me at the above address, or to the Borough Treasurer's Department, Howard Street, North Shields.

Yours sincerely,

Robert T. Smith

Mayor.

The captions read: "Show your strength by ringing the bell in one month and strike a blow for victory."

The £5,000 target was quickly reached and the money used in the war effort.

The Mascot

During the war there were always appeals for 'pennies' from the public for one fund or another, but none was more popular than the Spitfire Fund. A huge board was set up above the railings of Royal Jubilee School, on the corner of Albion Road and Preston Road just opposite Christ Church – my old school as an infant. The main hall became a British Restaurant during the war. A real Spitfire was standing in the grounds of Preston Towers at the top of Preston Road with another board appealing for pennies on the lawn of the premises.

I remember well the band of the airforce cadets marching down Preston Road. My wife told me that she went there to join, believing that there was a female equivalent cadet corp. However, she was told there was none (there was later) but that she could become their mascot if she liked. So Doreen Stoneman as she was then called became the only female in the Air Cadet Force of Great Britain, albeit that she was only the mascot. She was about 15 years old at the time. She tells me proudly that the cadets had their meetings in Preston Towers.

Right: The cover of a songsheet for the Borough of Tynemouth Spitfire Song.

Here are the lyrics of the Tynemouth song:

There's no need to take cover,
When you hear these engines sound;
British planes are in the skyways
On their daily vigil bound.
We'll make one of their number,
Write your name upon the wing;
When our plane is flying over
You will hear all Tynemouth sing:

Chorus

There's music in the sky
Don't you hear the engines humming?
Prepared to do or die.
The Tynemouth Plane is coming
Steadfast, reliant,
Spitfire or *Defiant*,
So give a rousing cheer,
The TYNEMOUTH PLANE is here!

Speeding over the Channel,
See the German bomber sail;
Limping back to Mr Goering
With a *Spitfire* on his tail.
Hitler, sitting in Munich,
Shouts to all his men of war,
"What's the noise about in Tynemouth?"
Then the Tynemouth people roar:

Repeat Chorus

THE BOROUGH OF TYNEMOUTH SPITFIRE SONG

Words and Music by
H. M. KING.

Price: SIXPENCE
All profits on the sale of this song are for Tynemouth Spitfire Fund

Dedicated to all British Airmen—especially Frank.

Cover drawn by
Master G. MEW.

The songsheets were sold for sixpence to raise money for the Spitfire Fund. On the inside of the songsheet is this advice: 'Towns may have copies of this song with their own names in place of "Tynemouth" if they are raising a plane themselves. Other counties too if their names fit.'

Other Fundraising

"WINGS FOR VICTORY" WEEK.

APRIL 3rd ——— APRIL 10th.

SALUTE TO THE R.A.F.

The Empress, Whitley Bay,

FRIDAY, APRIL 2nd, 7 p.m.
THURSDAY, APRIL 8th, 7 p.m.
} TWO PRESENTATIONS

ADMISSION FREE.   RESERVED SEATS 1/-.

Our Target is £250,000 — 50 Typhoons.

"INVEST IN THE R.A.F."

PROGRAMME — 2d.

Left: An advert of a concert to raise funds for 'Wings For Victory Week' – Salute to the RAF at The Empress, Whitley Bay.

Fundraising was a vital part of the war effort. Other campaigns included:

Warship Week

War Weapons Week

Tank Week

Salute the Soldier Week.

During one War Weapons Week a captured German Messerchmitt plane toured the North East.

My first jobs

Still during the war, between the ages of 14 and 16, I had a number of jobs for short intervals as an errand boy and paper boy. The first 'serious' job was at Tommy Wakefield's garage in Preston Avenue. Wakefield had by this time a large share in the Tynemouth Bus Company, so much so that a large number of buses running for that company still bore his name. His garage in Preston Avenue was a separate business and mainly garaged long distance lorries and funeral vehicles. He had also owned the charabancs which frequented the town in the days before the war. My main job was polishing cars and running messages. I remember wondering as I went to work if the garage had been hit by a bomb. But it never did. They were actually good employers. Tommy's son and daughter ran the business. Seppy (Septimus) was one of the long distance lorry drivers who seemed to have a permanent melancholy face that had fallen in, and he would tell me nonchalantly that he had just returned from Southampton or some other very distant part of Britain. I asked if I could go with him on the next trip and he said no. I often wondered how on earth these drivers could drive at night with only shaded headlights, lights that were covered with a mask with a number of slits, slanting the light down onto the road.

Wakefield's Workshop, Albion Road. Scarlet open topped charabancs used to line up outside Wakefield's waiting for trippers – a familiar sight in my day.

The Hell Ship *Altmark*

Before we come to the bombing of North Shields, there was an incident that created a lot of attention at the beginning of the war and has a connection with North Shields. It related to the discovery of a German prison ship that contained British seamen who were prisoners of war, and the conditions were said to be appalling. This ship became notorious as the hell ship *Altmark*. In mid-February the *Altmark* incident occurred. It was a supply ship for the scuttled pocket-battleship *Graf Spee*, sunk in December. The *Altmark* was returning to Germany and as a naval auxiliary ship she could legally claim freedom from search by foreign forces. However, she also had a large number of British merchant sailors on board from ships sunk by the *Graf Spee*. Once these men were in Germany, they would have been excellent propaganda fodder for the Nazi government at such an early stage in the war.

The Altmark in a Norwegian fjord.

On February 16th, 1940, the British cruiser *Arethusa* with the 4th Destroyer Flotilla intercepted the *Altmark* off the south coast of Norway. Two small Norwegian warships escorted the *Altmark* and they warned the British ships not to interfere with her. The commander of the 4th Flotilla received orders from the Admiralty to board the *Altmark* even though she had taken refuge in Norwegian waters. An offer was made that the *Altmark* could go to Bergen under escort where she would have been searched. However, when the destroyer *Cossack* tried to pull alongside the much larger *Altmark*, the supply ship attempted to ram the *Cossack*. In doing so, all the *Altmark* succeeded in doing was to run aground. British sailors rushed aboard her and freed the 299 merchant sailors who had been held on board. Among the 299 prisoners were two from North Shields, Thomas Hunter of Shiremoor and Raymond Atkinson of North Shields. The *Altmark* was re-floated at high tide and continued to Germany – minus her prize. Upon arrival home there were celebrations and ceremonies held in Jarrow, and North Shields.

Right: I show a picture of the released North Shields captives.

Chapter 3
Childhood Memories

Evacuation was not compulsory and many did not comply. For example, I cannot remember any of the near neighbours children being evacuated, certainly we were not, and nobody ever asked. I suppose with kids it seemed an exciting time and no one believed anything would happen to them. And yet, all around, we were getting news about someone's son being taken prisoner, shot down, or otherwise killed in action. There was a close neighbour whose son became a navigator in the air force, and I remember when he came home and all the kids wanted to see his half a wing on his uniform. Shortly afterwards he was reported missing over Germany and never returned. Being a seaport town, seamen were often reported missing believed lost at sea. In our street there were at least six merchant seaman, but I only remember one losing his life. But as for the evacuation of children, they left Tyneside by the hundred. My wife was evacuated to Rennington near Alnwick in, she believes, 1941. She certainly remembers a lot of the bombing, both the Wilkinson's Shelter Disaster and the bomb that fell on Waterville Road near her street. Of course Wilkinson's Shelter was hit on 4th May 1941 and Waterville Road on 1st October 1941.

Right: The cover of a public information leaflet from 1939 for 'Evacuation – Why and How'.

CIVIL DEFENCE

**EVACUATION
WHY AND HOW?**

PUBLIC INFORMATION
LEAFLET   NO. 3

Read   this   and
keep   it   carefully.
You may need it.

Issued from the Lord Privy Seal's Office **July, 1939**

This photograph of children being evacuated shows the gas mask boxes that everybody had to carry during the war, adults as well as children.

In the photo above are children of Percy Main Board School, the school attended by my wife Doreen. However, she said that because her father was a merchant seaman her mother kept them at home until the bombing got much worse, and had to organise the evacuation privately. Three sisters, among them Doreen's mother, took their children to Rennington, but I am told by Doreen, they were anything but happy. A serious and unfortunate incident was the catching of diphtheria by the youngest child of the family group. Doreen, being the eldest at eleven years old, took responsibility to fetch a doctor as the resident of the household thought it was nothing serious. There being no household telephone, Doreen had to borrow three pence to phone the doctor who, hearing the description of the illness came immediately and rushed the five year old child to hospital. Sadly Carol, the child, died shortly afterwards. Needless to say they all returned home. They had lost more when evacuated than they had at home.

Extracts from Monkseaton Secondary School's Log Book

4th September 1939
War having broken out yesterday between England and Germany, schools were closed for one week to the children. The staffs assembling as usual to await instructions.

11th September 1939
Closure of schools continued by order of the Education Committee until air raid shelters are completed.

22nd September 1939
Staff engaged today in visiting home address of every pupil on the registers to secure use of rooms in private residences and to notify children of sectional instruction therein. Gas mask inspection on 25th September 1939.

Operation Pied Piper – Evacuation of Children

The *Evening News* of Tuesday, September 5th 1939 gave details of the evacuation of children from the Borough of Tynemouth.

Departure Times Fixed and Destinations

Arrangements have now been completed for the evacuation of 1,908 school children from Tynemouth tomorrow. Destinations and numbers are Rothbury, 479; Bellingham, 206; Norham, 88; Belford, 255; Wooler, 366; Morpeth, 444; and Hexham, 70. Children must assemble at schools and no child will be allowed to join the school party at the station. All entrain at North Shields Station with the exception of the Percy Main unit which leaves Percy Main Station.

Percy Main Station – a starting point for many evacuees leaving for the country. This view is from before the war.

Following are details for each unit:

School	Approx No of Evacuees	Time to meet at School	Time to arrive Station	Train departs at	Destination Station
KING EDWARD UNIT		7.15	8.15	8.30	Rothbury
King Edward Boys	105				
Girls	92				
Infants	25				
Priory Mixed	66				
Infants	25				
ROMAN CATHOLIC UNIT		7.15	8.15	8.30	Rothbury
St Joseph's	78				
St Cuthbert's	88				
RALPH GARDNER UNIT		7.15	8.15	8.30	Bellingham
Ralph Gardner Boys	83				
Girls	71				
Spring Gardens Mixed	40				
Infants	9				
Open All School	2				
Lovain House	1				
PERCY MAIN UNIT		11.00	12.05	12.20	Tweedmouth Station and proceed by bus to Norham
Ridges	1				
Chirton	2				
Collingwood	1				
Percy Main Mixed	33				
Infants	22				
Percy St John's	29				

Boys exercising at Queen Victoria School around the time of the war. Lads like these were evacuated to Wooler.

		11.15	12.25	12.40	
WESTERN UNIT		11.15	12.25	12.40	Belford
Western Boys	120				
Girls	89				
Infants	46				
QUEEN VICTORIA UNIT		11.15	12.25	12.40	Wooler
Western Boys	55				
Girls	49				
Infants	48				
EASTERN UNIT		11.15	12.25	12.40	Wooler
Eastern Boys	38				
Girls	37				
Infants	33				
Christ Church Boys	61				
Girls	30				
St Oswin Infants	15				
LINSKILL UNIT		12.15	1.15	1.30	Morpeth
Linskill Boys	188				
Girls	256				
SECONDARY SCHOOL UNIT		1.45	2.50	3.05	Hexham
Municipal High	70				
Grand total	1908				

Children accompanied by one of their parents attended schools this afternoon for the purpose of having their kit inspected and to receive final instructions.

A quiet view of Belford before the war – the village where I live. This would have been a peaceful environment for evacuees used to the busy town of North Shields.

Canny Old Shields
by Norman Christenson

Norman Christenson wrote his memories of growing up in his home town of North Shields – Canny Old Shields he called it – in the book *Plodgin' Through The Clarts*. Here he remembers the bombing of the Second World War:

All of us very quickly became air raid experts. Even the youngest of us, after a relatively short time, could confidently pick the difference between the drumming roar of our own planes, and the deep thrum thrum thrum of the German's. We could also differentiate between artillery fire and bombing, and, as we became even more expert, we could tell fairly accurately whether the descending whistle indicated a comfortably distant bomb blast, a reasonably close one or one that had us with our heads between our legs waiting for imminent explosion. Being imbued with the usual childlike faith in our own immortality, even the closest of close calls was treated as nothing more than yet another adventure to regale our mates with on the morrow.

But if the bombs didn't worry us, the time certainly did. Our concern in this regard stemmed from the fact that we got the following morning off school if the all clear sounded after midnight. And so our parents, who may have been slightly distracted by the bombs dropping all around them, were driven out even closer to distraction by our constant enquiries about what time it was. Only posh people like those in Tynemouth owned proper wrist watches but one of the women invariably grabbed the family alarm clock on their exit from the house and this was continuously checked until either the all clear went to our groans at five to or to our collective sighs at five past midnight.

When we did have a late night and the resultant morning off, we'd be out on the streets bright and early in the quest for shrapnel. Every kid had a box or bag in which they stored their treasured collection of the twisted metal pieces that could be heard clunking onto tiles and roadways at the height of the raids. These would be endlessly examined and appraised and swapped and bartered like so many of the other totally useless things we saved and treasured. A set of tail fins off a German incendiary bomb was the pride of my not inconsiderable collection. This fell through the roof of the Stutt's house one night and only the prompt action of Mr Stutt, who quelled it under the contents of a strategically placed sand bag, restricted the damage to a hole burned in the middle of a rug. I'm not sure how I came to possess this prize ahead of the three Stutt's kids but I probably swapped it for some hardly-used chewing gum or a reasonable sized apple gowk. Many houses did of course come to a more fiery or explosive end than the Stutt's place and these provided a whole new array of playgrounds. Boring old parks with their swings and roundabouts were no match for the bomb sites that abounded. Half demolished staircases still clinging precariously to garishly wallpapered walls became our Mount Everest as we clambered up them, ignoring the bits and pieces of mortar-covered brick that disintegrated around us. Piles of rubble quickly became forts or gun emplacements from which we sallied forth rat tat tatting at the 'Nazis' occupying the cream and green remains of a kitchen where some wife recently tried to turn four ounces of lap into a tasty meal for six. More exotic ruins like the rat-infested old warehouses down Borough Bank or the ruined church opposite gave us a veritable wonderland of creaking rafters, fallen floors, gaping roofs and sagging doors

Norman Christenson as a boy in North Shields.

Norman's class at Queen Victoria School around 1939.

were all the more attractive because they were so strictly forbidden. It never dawned on us that a lot of poor souls had been uprooted and sometimes killed to provide our amusement areas but we were only kids making the most of what was to us a normal state of affairs.

Although it was mainly the older parts of Shields that bore the brunt of the air raids, we had our own near misses in The Ridges, no doubt as the German High Command tried once more to get the nearby gas works. A fair bit of Chirton disappeared on one memorable night when a parachute-born mine set off an explosion that rocked us in our shelter over half a mile away. The target of this attack was obviously The Rex cinema where Wor Ma subsequently spent the best years of her life waiting for that last elusive Bingo number. Sat in our shelter one night not long after this earth-shaking incident, we soon realised that tonight's raid was to be one of the heaviest we'd experienced. Through a slight crack in the tarpaulin door cover, we could see reflected in our front room window, the harsh white light from the search lights that criss-crossed the sky, interspersed with flashes as bombs struck and the flickering red of the ensuing flames. The bombers seemed to drone on and on and on, harried always by the anti-aircraft guns that kept up a furious clatter and sent a veritable rainstorm of shrapnel clattering all around. Amid all this background din, we were suddenly aware that the next whistling bomb was much closer than any of the preceding lot and, more importantly, was getting closer by the second. Mr Stutt who'd been giving a running commentary from the door must have arrived at the same conclusion as he started frantically tugging at the tarpaulin to get inside. The bomb beat him by about half a second. An almighty explosion shook the shelter as though it were in the grip of a major earthquake, the women screamed, the sound of shattering glass was everywhere, Derek, my brother, flew out of the top bunk and Mr Stutt arrived in a tangle of arms and legs and dust and cordite fumes. Deafened by the noise it seemed at first as if someone had turned off the volume control until slowly, the sounds of the now diminishing raid and a relative silence returned.

We emerged after the all clear to survey the damage. The offending bomb had landed on the pavement on the other side of Silkey's Lane, leaving a fair sized crater and an electric lamp post that leaned over it as if it were inspecting the damage. The front of our block had taken the full force of the explosion that had shattered every pane of glass, sending lethal shards through the lacerated blackout curtains that flapped in tatters around the jagged window frames. Inside, the scene was even worse. Crunching our way over the layer of broken glass, we shielded candles to check a sight that must have been heartbreaking to someone as house proud as Wor Ma. The battered interior was covered in a fine layer of soot dislodged from the chimney by the blast. Everywhere we walked and everything we touched was coated with a mixture of glass particles and soot and left that acrid coaly smell that stayed on long after every nook and cranny had been scrubbed and mopped back to some semblance of order. Council men came the next day and filled in the bomb hole and pushed the lamp post back straight, others worked with panes of glass and putty to restore our windows and those of our neighbours, others fixed loose roof tiles and in a relatively short time our street had returned to normal or as normal as you can get when people are dropping bombs on you.

The German High Command made one more attempt to get either us or the gas works. With the last experience still fresh in our minds, we cringed as the descending bombs whistled closer and closer and closer until their banshee wail seemed they were almost on top of us. Bracing ourselves for the inevitable we crouched in the approved fashion, heads between our legs and hands squashing our ears to our heads as we braced for the shock and explosion that never came. What we got instead was a series of crumping thumps that were felt rather than heard. The mystery was solved early the next morning when a tin hatted policeman rat tatted on our door and explained that we would have to be evacuated until a squad of soldiers disarmed the bombs that had fallen all around us but failed to explode. So much for the famous German super efficiency! Our faces lit up at these glad tidings. We were off to the country where we'd ride horses, chase sheep, climb haystacks and sleep in great soft eiderdowned beds and have eggs every day plus our own Ma to look after us. Unfortunately this wasn't quite the sort of evacuation they had in mind as we soon discovered when Ma dragged us and a few belongings two streets away to Uncle Tom's in Laburnum Avenue where we somehow squeezed into an already crowded house for the few days it took the army to remove the bombs. This episode brought about our sole family casualty when Whiskers, one of our innumerable family cats, disappeared during the upheaval, never to return. It also created some brand new playgrounds in the shape of a few additional craters to the already pockmarked surface of the front field which was rapidly taking on a distinctly lunar appearance.

The raids gradually subsided after this last intensive campaign and the nightly alarms became things of the past as the town set about clearing up the debris and returning to some sort of normality. While Shields never had to endure the massive

raids that other major cities suffered from, we still had more than our fair share of damage, traumas and tragedies. The worst of these, by far, was the Wilkinson's disaster. Wilkinson's bottled soft drinks in their factory in the older east end of town and one of the large cellars beneath the factory, acted as a shelter for many of the people who occupied the adjacent houses. It received a direct hit during one of the heavier raids and the neighbourhood was decimated, and the entire town left mourning, as whole families died in the resulting carnage.

Norman Christenson later emigrated to Australia and here he is left on a return to his home town in 1994. He is outside 9 Laburnum Avenue – his home in North Shields fifty years before.

Chapter 4
The Bombing of North Shields

Strange as it may sound, North Shields was a sizeable town of over 50,000 inhabitants at the time of the war, yet its administrative body was given the name of one of its minor districts, Tynemouth – a small, picturesque village beside the sea and at the mouth of the River Tyne on the outskirts of the 'borough' which eventually became Tynemouth County Borough. Consequently during the war, all references to North Shields come under the umbrella of Tynemouth County Borough which had its own chief constable and the whole paraphernalia of Civil Defence within its boundaries. The town hall and council offices were in North Shields, the police headquarters and fire brigade was just around the corner, the main library, telephone exchange, shopping centre and the industries such as the fishing industry, Smith's Dock and a major wood yard that supplied the many coal pits in the area with pit props all were in North Shields. From the time Tynemouth had its baptism of fire with its first bomb, there followed a total of 329 such incidents; during which three Tynemouth policemen were killed: P.C. Clements, First Reserve Murray and First Reserve Hannah.

Here is an account of the early bombings in North Shields from the *North East Diary 1939-1945* website by Roy Ripley and Brian Pears.

Friday, 9th & Saturday, 10th August 1940
An HE on the railway north of Cullercoats station and three in fields west of Broadway. Some property damage.

Sunday, 12th May 1940
A stray Barrage balloon damaged seventeen houses at Tynemouth. This incident alone shows the potential for damage to the German raiders. London would have suffered even heavier damage had it not been for these 'silver elephants' of the air.

Tuesday, 18th June 1940
Churchill's speech given today 'This Was Their Finest Hour'. This quotation includes the famous phrase: "What General Weygand called the Battle of France is over. I expect that the Battle of Britain is about to begin. Let us therefore brace ourselves to our duties, and so bear ourselves that, if the British Empire and its Commonwealth last for a thousand years, men will say, "This was their finest hour".

Tuesday, 2nd July 1940
Newcastle and Jarrow were attacked during the late afternoon. The damage was considerable. A single German Dornier bomber passed over Blaydon, shot down a balloon and dropped bombs on Newcastle and Co Durham. Jarrow: Fourteen dead and 120 injured. Three HEs dropped in streets. Four houses and six flats demolished, and

Extracts from Monkseaton Secondary School's Log Book

29th January 1940
Air raid warning sounded at 10.20. Shelters occupied for approximately $\frac{1}{2}$ hour.

13th May 1940
Acting on Friday's wireless instructions cancelling Whit holidays school reassembled this Monday morning. Later wireless instructions calling up 'neutral' schools for Tuesday, led to confusion resulting in attendance of 94 children only out of 282 and absence of 3 teachers out of 12. After discovering that the other schools in the area had closed, this school was dismissed at 10.15 so no registers were marked.

six houses and thirty flats damaged. School partly collapsed. Three domestic shelters and five others damaged. Four or five streets were affected but most casualties occurred in Princess Street, a search of the debris for trapped victims went on throughout the night, firemen, ARP workers and others working in relays. It was announced that the August Bank Holiday is to be cancelled.

My Memories

I remember that day in early July 1940 very well. It was overcast with low cloud and rain threatening. I was delivering newspapers with my brother Ian in Percy Main when we heard this 'thrum thrum thrum', a well known sound by now of a German bomber which appeared to be flying low overhead. People on the street were looking upwards when a 'flying pencil', as Dornier bombers were nicknamed because of their slim pencil like appearance, suddenly broke out of the clouds flying very low, so low in fact that you could see the airmen inside the aircraft. While this may sound far-fetched it became the talk of the town later as many people had seen the airmen looking out of the cockpit windows. Many years later, when I was discussing this with my wife, she told me (without me suggesting it) "I could see the pilot looking down". The plane was flying towards the river and disappeared in cloud when we heard a short whistle and a very loud thud. We dashed for the shelters which were nearby. They were what we called street shelters, large brick blocks with very heavy concrete roofs. We had vowed never to go inside one as they appeared to be death traps but we were afraid of our own shrapnel from the anti-aircraft guns which had now began firing.

A few more bombs dropped and after about twenty minutes the all-clear sounded. We knew from the direction just across the river that the bombs had fallen either on Hebburn or Jarrow. Later that evening we were told that a factory in Jarrow had been hit and that 11 women had been killed. Until a report was published in 2001 I had no idea of the truth of the matter except that we did know the bomber was a lone raider as we called them. In fact the time shown is precise, eleven minutes after 6pm the normal time we would finish our paper round. We got to know nothing officially about casualties during the war but the rumours were never far from the mark.

Local newspapers printed Government safety advice for bombing raids:

Yourself

Examine your gas mask and carry it with you always.

Carry your identity card everywhere.

Always wear your identity disc.

Be sure of your Warden's address and positions of First Aid Posts, local shelters and branch Fire Stations.

Your Home

See your black-out is perfect.

Protect your windows.

Clear all rubbish from top floor.

Have buckets of sand and long-handled shovels in readiness to deal with incendiary bombs.

Your air raid shelter should be earthed to depths 16 inches top, 30 inches at sides and have protected entrance.

Air Raids

When the siren sounds take cover.

If at home turn off electricity and gas.

If there is overhead firing but no siren take shelter away from danger of flying glass.

Don't leave home shelter for street shelter.

Don't use telephone unnecessarily.

The Greatest Day
Thursday, 15th August 1940

The *North East Diary 1939-1945* website by Roy Ripley and Brian Pears reports:

Today was probably the most significant day in the Battle of Britain as far as the north-east is concerned ... The man to whom the North-East is indebted for the successful defence of this area has not had very much in the way of recognition, he was the Air Officer Commanding, 13 Group, Air Vice-Marshal Richard Ernest Saul, DFC.

Despite enthusiastic claims made by the RAF (182 shot down), the true total of German losses was still a crushing blow to them. Over the whole country, seventy-five lost and a further fifteen returning to base damaged. They also lost a further three planes and damaged another five in accidents. The majority of people living in the North-East on this August day did not really know much about the events of the day ...

Only five days later, Winston Churchill paid tribute to the efforts of the Royal Air Force: "The gratitude of every home in our island, in our Empire and indeed throughout the world, except in the abodes of the guilty, goes out to the British airmen who, undaunted by odds, unwearied in their constant challenge and mortal danger, are turning the tide of world war by their prowess and by their devotion. Never in the field of human conflict was so much owed by so many to so few."

My Memories

On one notable afternoon, the sound of distance machine-gun fire and the roar of fighter engines brought out hundreds into the street. The actual battle seemed to be just over the coast and it lasted several hours. We all rushed for the shelters when a bomber would detach itself from the fray and head up the Tyne. Later that evening my brother Ian who worked in the dispatch office of the Shields Evening News, said that one of their reporters had been standing in the doorway of Stoniers the Chemist in Nile Street, North Shields when machine-gun bullets from an aircraft ripped into the doorpost. He later said there had been a major battle over the sea.

Riverside Firefighters wearing their full equipment.

The Gambling School

The *North East Diary* reports on 10th/11th October 1940 that a UXB landed in the Tynemouth area between Coast Road and Flatworth Gambling School.

The above named Gambling School was a well known area locally called John Pie Hill. I have no idea how it derived the name or how it is spelt. It was located on a footpath from Percy Main to Willington Square on ground belonging to Flatworth Farm and was by this time only raised ground full of what appeared to be small craters but ideal for any clandestine business. They were high enough and deep enough to hide a 'hoyin(g) school' which in the common vernacular means pitch and toss. To hoy anything on Tyneside is to throw something, such as throwing pennies in the air and someone to shout either heads or tails. A number of my mates at the pit attended this 'school' (I like the word) and they used to vow that it was the fairest form of gambling. After all they would argue "All you have to do is shout 'heads' and if it lands heads up you win the kitty." Heads you win, tails you lose, it couldn't be simpler or fairer than that. I used to wonder therefore how more often than not they came back skint. I remember on a Sunday when kids used to go for a walk in the fields that John Pie Hill was the

objective to see if we could see the 'school' getting raided by police. It would never have happened. When we kids approached, a man's head would pop up and he would say "Scram". He was one of the many touts 'employed' by the school's hierarchy to protect their interests. It was a whispered secret that some of the police had a protection racket, in other words, "Pay up and we will keep away."

An wonderful illustration of pitch and toss by Vera Hook.

Extracts from Monkseaton Secondary School's Log Book

20th June 1940
Attendance declined from 96% yesterday to 86% today owing to an air raid alarm from 11.45 pm to 3 am many children having experienced a disturbing night. No local bombing or gunfire.

27th August 1940
Air raid alarm lasting $5^1/_2$ hours last night. Attendance only 71% this morning, rising to 90% in afternoon.

29th August 1940
Air raid attack last night resulting in severe damage to school premises, the school was closed (without assembly) this morning until further notice.

2nd September 1940
School re-opened after an interval of two days. Several rooms not yet ready, but emergency arrangements as to timetable have been made to ensure full time working for the whole of the pupils. Air raid last night. 191 children present this morning out of 285. Afternoon attendance 223.

Wednesday, 9th/Thursday, 10th April 1941

A report to the Emergency Committee by the Chief Constable and ARP Controller, Tom Blackburn, dated 17th April 1941.

I have to inform you that at 23.25 on the 9th April, 1941, the public warning was sounded in this Borough. The 'Raiders Passed' signal was given at 04.50 on the 10th April, 1941. During the $5^1/_2$ hours the warning was in operation enemy aircraft flew over the Borough at intervals, and there was heavy anti-aircraft gunfire during the whole period. The raid commenced with a shower of IB in the high part of the town, and a small number of HE were dropped. Between 00.30 and 01.30 more IB and HE were dropped at intervals at the Timber Storage Yards and Docks at the riverside, and in the centre of the town, the raid ended with a further shower of IB and HE mainly on the Timber Yards and Docks. So far as can be ascertained 35 HE, mainly of heavy calibre, fell and exploded, and thousands of IB were dropped. A large number of the latter failed to ignite and quite a good proportion of them were of the explosive type, one of which caused a fatality.

No. 3.—Chief Constable and A.R.P. Controll- (Mr Tom Blackburn)

A cartoon of Chief Constable Tom Blackburn.

'With the exception of the bombs dropped at Maple Crescent, The Quadrant, Cartington Road and Biddlestone Crescent, all the HE dropped were of a very heavy calibre. The craters averaged 70' to 80' across and 25' deep. The blast effect from these bombs was tremendous and far reaching. The four bombs mentioned as exceptions to the very heavy ones were of a medium type, with craters about 25' across and 3' to 8' deep. The blast effect in these instances was very great having regard to the size of the craters. Of the heavy bombs above mentioned, five were of an exceptionally heavy type. The craters being in the vicinity of 120' across and 30' to 35' deep. Numerous reports of UXB were received but none were concerned with property. A thorough search was made as early as possible after the 'Raiders Passed' had been sounded, but none of the reports were confirmed.

At Biddlestone Crescent, an Anderson Shelter received what must have been a direct hit, and the occupants were killed instantly, the adjoining home being completely destroyed, but an Anderson Shelter five yards away was undamaged and the occupants unhurt.

A member of one of the squads who would cut up defused unexploded bombs.

My Memories

During the war I worked for a jobbing builder called Jimmy Dixon and one of our jobs was to tile a bathroom in Alma Place, North Shields for a Mrs Rosie Tuffle who had a small newsagents shop on Howdon Road. As I was not yet sixteen, I worked as an 'improver' with the tiler who I think was called Arthur Eggleston. Anyway he said he was nineteen years old so he must have been an apprentice. He said to me, "Do you know who I am?" I was puzzled and I said no. "Do you remember a bomb falling behind the Pineapple Inn and killing four people who were in an Anderson shelter, but one person survived?" I certainly did. This was the talk of the town for a week. What I remembered was the amazing escape of a lad who was also in the shelter. I must have gaped at him and he said "That was me." He then told me that the deaths were not from a direct hit but from bomb blast that sucked the air from the victims' lungs. For some reason it missed this young man. "I had all the clothes torn from my body", he said. This was in the local paper at the time shown as 'An amazing escape from death' or words to that affect. Naturally I have never forgotten that incident. To actually be talking to this survivor was an amazing event.

My Memories

Also on this day, Willington Quay was badly hit. My dad had relations living there and he told us (the lads) to have a walk there and see if Aunty Alice, who's husband was at sea, was ok. Ian, my brother, and I walked to Howdon and as we were going along the path towards Willington Quay, I was amazed to meet Auntie Alice and her two children carrying a few belongings. I noticed that her eye now had a bad cast that she didn't have before. She told us that her brother was believed dead, blown up by a land mine. Apparently he had been fire-watching and saw a parachute falling, and believing it was an airman, he and another man ran towards it. However, it was a land mine that blew up on contact with the earth. Years later she told me that her brother's Identity Card had been found riddled with holes in the dock near where she lived. The houses damaged in her street were later demolished. Five people were rescued alive from the debris at Willington Quay, but a fifteen year old boy died after rescue.

Biddlestone Crescent, showing troops involved in sifting through the pieces of Anderson shelter destroyed by the bomb.

The official report continues:

RESCUE SERVICES. The Rescue and Demolition Service was called out to seven incidents, the Repair Service to two, and at one incident the Decontamination Squad performed rescue work. In addition, two Rescue Squads from Wallsend and one from Whitley Bay were sent for and despatched to incidents. The above services represented by fifteen parties, were tireless in their efforts and were able to rescue alive eleven persons trapped and recover fifteen bodies from debris. The last body was recovered at 23.00 on Saturday night. At the Stanley Street West incident, a number of persons who were provided with Domestic Surface Shelters, took refuge in their houses, and a number of them would doubtless have been alive had they taken cover in these shelters. This was demonstrated by the shelters which were standing when the properties in the vicinity had been razed to the ground. One couple had taken refuge under a dining room table, on top of which a piano had been thrown, resulting in the collapse of the table. It was noticeable that the whole of the plaster in the ceilings and walls of the totally demolished houses was disintegrated to fine dust and some of the bodies taken out were actually buried in this powdered plaster. At the Institution two Surface Shelters, each for fifty persons, one of which was on the edge of the crater, suffered no damage and the occupants were unharmed.

CASUALTIES. In the course of the raid, 35 persons were killed, these consist of 17 adult males, 13 adult females, and 5 children under 16 years. Reports received up the present show that 101 persons were injured as follows:

	Men	Women	Children
Seriously Injured	10	4	1
Slightly Injured	62	15	9

Of the persons killed there was one soldier, one Police Constable, one First Police Reserve (Ex Inspector), and one male and one female of the Whitley Bay First Aid Services. Of the persons seriously injured, there was one Police Constable, one Special Constable and five Civil Defence Personnel. Of the persons slightly injured, there were two Police Sergeants, two Police Constables, three Special Constables and thirteen Civil Defence Personnel.

DAMAGE. The following is a resume of the damage caused to buildings so far as can be ascertained at the present.

Totally demolished	22
So badly damaged that demolition was necessary	41
Seriously damaged but repairable	99
Slightly damaged exclusive of glass	513

A Union Jack flies in Cartington Road after the raid on 10th April 1941.

Severe damage after the raid on 10th April 1941.

FIRES. IB (Incendiary Bombs) caused numerous small fires in the timber storage yards. These developed into five major fires and later into a conflagration, which extended for about one mile along the river front to the west of the main part of the town. Every effort was made to extinguish the conflagration before dark on the 10th instant, and the situation was well in hand but at about 10.00 a breeze sprang up and increased the danger. At 10.30 Mr C. Thomas, the Regional Fire Inspector, arrived and took charge of this incident. He called for assistance and aiding parties, consisting of two units (each) arrived from Newburn, Gosforth and Blyth. Military Assistance was also obtained and the soldiers were employed removing timber from the danger area. By 14.00 the fire was under control and extinguished at 18.00.

At about the same time as the timber yards were becoming a serious matter, three large fires developed very rapidly in the centre of the town, involving three large shops within a space of 80 yards. The water supply was insufficient because of the nearness of the buildings, and it was obvious that extra pumping appliances for relaying water would have to be obtained. At 03.23 I requested Whitley Bay Control to send all available fire appliances to assist in fighting fires which had developed, they replied that nine units would be immediately despatched. These arrived quickly, and the fires referred to above were soon under control. The fire float was also brought into operation for these incidents to pump water from the river. They were extinguished at 07.00 when the Whitley Bay aiding party was released.

In addition several hundreds of small fires were started in all parts of the town, and these were speedily dealt with by the Fire Service, Police, Wardens and Civilians who tackled bombs as they fell, saving, without doubt, hundreds of properties. Over 100 calls were received at the Fire Station and it is estimated that at least 400 minor fires were dealt with. The Mobile Water Carriers recently acquired by the Fire Authority proved invaluable during the course of the raid in dealing with fires where the water was off or the supply insufficient. The fact that only one pump failed is indicative of the manner in which the appliances stood up to the test. In all, forty-three appliances were used from this Brigade, and fifteen aiding Units were employed in dealing with fires. At 03.00 the position regarding the fires was giving cause for anxiety, by 04.00 the position had eased, at all other times the situation was well in hand.

COMMUNICATIONS. At 01.30 practically all police box telephones were out of order, and many of the exchange lines from Fire Stations, Wardens Posts and other Depots, were damaged, or inoperative, and the Messenger Services were brought into operation. I wish to specially mention the Messenger Service for the excellent duties that they carried out during this period which enabled communications to be maintained between the Control Centre and the various Services. During the raid the emergency telephone exchange was put into operation which curtailed the telephone facilities available for all services. A permanent call to the Regional Office was arranged by the Post Office Engineer in order that direct communication could be made to that office as to the progress of the raid.

FIRST AID. This Service was fully extended, and I obtained assistance from Whitley Bay for this work. Unfortunately on the arrival of one vehicle of this service a bomb dropped on First Aid Headquarters at 'Holmlands' killing one female and one male personnel of the aiding detachment. This service functioned extremely satisfactorily despite several unanticipated difficulties which were: extensive damage to the Casualty Service Control Office, to the 'Holmlands' First Aid Post and the loss of several vehicles resulting from varied degrees of damage sustained. At no time during the raid was any branch of the Service depleted to such an extent as to render it ineffective. The total number of calls made on the service was:

Ambulances	34
First Aid Parties	22
Cars for sitting cases	14

The number of casualties passing through First Aid Posts was as follows:

Holmlands	37
Balkwell	6
Royal Naval Sick Bay	5

The number of casualties admitted to hospital were:

Preston Hospital	41 of which 6 were dead
Tynemouth Hospital	21 of which 8 were dead

As a result of First Aid Headquarters and Holmlands First Aid Post being put out of action, on the following day arrangements were made for the use of Smith's Dock Institute as a Central First Aid Post, and was ready to be put into operation in a satisfactory manner on the following night.

Holmlands First Aid Post destroyed with Christ Church parish church in the background.

DAMAGE TO ESSENTIAL SERVICES. It is most fortunate that these services were damaged in very few instances, and no serious inconvenience was experienced. Although Gas, Water and Electric Mains were damaged at one incident, the services were quickly restored temporarily. The telephone cable was damaged at one incident which was responsible for failing the telephone communications.

MILITARY AID. Military Aid was requested to assist at the timber yard fire, 100 troops were engaged in this work and their services were invaluable, saving large quantities of timber. A further 100 troops assisted in cordoning damaged areas and guarding damaged premises to prevent looting. All these troops were supplied by the MC Holding Battalion, stationed at Prudhoe Convalescent Homes, Whitley Bay. I also requested assistance from the Officer Commanding the Troop Stations locally, to assist in dealing with the clearing of debris from highways, and rescue work.

Prudhoe Convalescent Home, Whitley Bay – where troops were stationed during the war.

LOOTING. Only one case of looting was reported. A Special Constable detained a boy of twelve years for stealing from a house damaged by war operations. This boy is to be summoned under the Defence Regulations.

AFTER CARE. As a result of the raid many persons have been rendered homeless. The majority of these were admitted to Emergency Feeding Centres. "Youth Centre" Rest Centre was opened at 00.05 on Thursday, 10th April, 1941, and closed at 21.45 on Saturday, 12th April, 1941, the total number on the register being 224, which includes eight transferred from the Western Rest Centre on being closed. The "Western" Rest Centre opened at 03.00 on the 10th April, and closed at 19.55 on the 11th April, 1941, the total number on the register being sixty-three. The total dealt with at both centres being 279. In addition to these a good number of persons rendered homeless made their own arrangements for billeting.

POLICE AND SPECIAL CONSTABLES. The members of the Police Force and Special Constabulary carried out their duties in an extremely efficient manner, assisting all services and taking control of incidents, and were largely responsible for maintaining the morale of the general public.

WARDENS SERVICE. The Wardens Service rendered invaluable service during the whole of the raid by assisting the Police and Firemen in their duties, by rendering First Aid to casualties, and by rescuing persons from damaged buildings prior to the arrival of the Rescue Service.

INDUSTRIAL UNDERTAKINGS. Messrs Smith's Dock Co Ltd. A number of IB fell on these premises which were effectively dealt with by their own ARP Services. Messrs Cookson's Lead & Antimony Co Ltd. A number of IB fell upon the premises of this firm which were effectively dealt with by their ARP Services. Gas Co. Three HE were dropped on the premises of the Gas Co, and about 200 IB. One HE caused damage to the railway lines leading from the main line into the Gas Co.'s premises. The IB were dealt with by their own services, some of which fell upon a Gas Holder burning holes in one of the Holders.

Tyne Improvement Commission. Fifteen HE in addition to IB which have already been reported, fell on the premises of the TIC Docks and Timber Yards. Buildings and houses were damaged by a fire, and the permanent way and lines were blocked and damaged in various parts of the Docks and Timber Yards. A considerable number of railway trucks were also damaged.

INFORMATION BUREAU. An Information Bureau was opened immediately after the raid at the Town Clerk's Office, Tynemouth, which has been operating very effectively.

GENERAL. There was a grand response from volunteers reporting for duty, and all Civil Defence personnel worked with a will, speed and efficiency which merited the confidence which has been placed in them. They carried out their duties under very trying conditions. It is very gratifying to report that the civilian population stood up to the conditions remarkably well, and at no time was there any suggestion of panic. The manner in which the IB were dealt with by the Services and general public is worthy of the highest praise. I wish to express my appreciation for the able and valuable assistance rendered to me by the Officials of all Services.

The damage caused by the attack of 10th April 1941. In the first air raid to cause casualties in the Borough of Tynemouth thirty three high explosive bombs were dropped.

Report to the Emergency Committee from the Town Clerk, 17th April, 1941:

GENERAL INFORMATION CENTRE. Immediately after the "Raiders Passed' signal sounded on the morning of the 10th April, 1941, the Town Clerks Office was opened as a General Information Centre, and information was supplied to all enquirers throughout the day until 19.30. Information relating to missing relatives, repairs to property, removal and salvage of furniture, funeral arrangements and general advice was available to persons needing assistance. The office remained open each day from 09.00 until 18.30 on the Friday, Saturday, Sunday, Monday and Tuesday following the raid.

On Thursday, the 10th April, approximately 400 enquires were dealt with, and the total number in connection with the raid during the period referred to amounted to approximately 850. Lists were prepared of persons requiring repairs to their property, and these were forwarded to the Borough Surveyor for his attention. Similar lists were prepared for cases requiring billeting or for furniture salvage or removal.

CASUALTY INFORMATION BUREAU. The Casualty Information Bureau obtained the necessary particulars relating to injured and dead from hospitals and mortuaries, and lists were published outside the Town Clerk's Office and the Police Station. Relatives of dead persons were traced and notified by post or messenger.

MORTUARY. Immediately after the raid, the Church Way Mortuary was opened, and nineteen bodies were received. All the bodies were identified, though in many cases considerable difficulty was experienced in finding relatives and in obtaining sufficient evidence to enable identification to be carried out. The utmost credit should be given to Mr Arthur Cragg, the Honorary Mortuary Superintendent, for his untiring work in a difficult and distressing task. Arrangements were made for the funerals of the victims to be carried out by the Corporation where the relatives were unable or unwilling to do so. The total number buried by the Corporation was twenty-three. This number was drawn, not merely from the Church Way Mortuary, but also from Preston Hospital and the Tynemouth Victoria Jubilee Infirmary.

SALVAGE OF FURNITURE. The scheme for the removal and salvage of furniture from damaged property was put into operation the morning after the raid and has been carried on in a very efficient manner under the direction of the Honorary Salvage Officer, Mr J. Duffy. The total number of cases where property was removed amounted to fifty. Of this number, twenty-two were placed in storage by the Corporation. For this purpose, St Andrew's Hall, the basement of the Liberal Club, a portion of Bishopsgate House and certain empty rooms at Queen Victoria School were taken over.

Bombed Out

The following was advice given out by the Ministry of Home Security for those who were 'bombed out':

See those friends today

... and make plans to go and stay with them, or for *them* to come and stay with *you*, if either of your houses is knock out.

Help is ready

If you can't make your own arrangements and you have to leave your home to go to a Rest Centre. Ask your warden where one is. There you will get food and clothes and somewhere to sleep. You will be given advice on your problems and help in finding a new home.

If your gas is cut off

There may be a communal feeding centre nearby, where you can get hot meals at very low prices. Find out about it, and if there isn't one, fix up to eat with friends or relations.

Ocean View, Whitley Bay, following the dropping of two land mines on 16th April 1941.

A view of bombed housing at St George's Road, Cullercoats, probably after the raid on 11th/12th October 1942 when six people were killed.

Blackthorn Crescent Memories

I am sure it was on the day when Silkey's Lane was hit, that the nearest bomb to our house fell on Blackthorn Crescent. While on the phone to my brother Ken in Sheffield recently, telling him about the book, he said to me quite involuntarily, "Have you mentioned Blackthorn Crescent?" He said this because we were all aware at the time, even though he was four years younger than me, how near a squeak it had been for us. But it is not shown on the official records. However the story of that night ensures that the memory will live on. As I have said before, my father was a veteran of the Boer War and was wounded in the knee on Spion Kop, South Africa. He also served in the First

World War in France and in particular fought in the Battle of Arras. Therefore, perhaps he was showing us his bravery rather than foolhardiness as my mother called it, for refusing to come into the Anderson Shelter with us. He probably thought he was keeping our spirits up. On this particular night he was in bed when the raid started. He refused to get up. My mother ushered us into the shelter and went back to plead with him, to no avail.

We listened to the noise of gunfire, watched the flaming onions tracing their way into the sky, saw the flares from the planes lighting up the whole area and then heard the dreaded whistle of the bombs that shuddered into the ground. "My God, they were close" said my mother. They had hit Silkey's Lane and Rose Cottage (see picture below). Then there was an almighty "Wham!" and the shelter shook. We had all ducked instinctively as though it would have made any difference. Before we had even regained our senses, we heard the clambering into the shelter, of 'Dad the Brave' who said, "The bloody ceiling fell on the bed." Blackthorn Crescent had been hit which was very close to our street. This was the closest to us than any other bomb that fell during the war. Quite a lot of bombs fell in that raid but Dad never stayed in the house during an air raid again.

My dad, John Ross Curran, a miner of the old school, born 1876 in Annbank, Ayrshire, Scotland. He was a soldier in the Boer War (1899-02), fought in the First World War (1914-18), and in Dad's Army, the Home Guard, (1939-45).

A picture of Rose Cottage, situated at the bottom of Silkey's Lane. It was believed that a man had lost an eye because of the bomb blast but this was never confirmed. I came to know Rose Cottage very well after the war. I was then engaged to Doreen and while at her house in Hazelwood Avenue, her dad would jump

on his bike and race to put a bet on at Rose Cottage, then hurry back to listen to the race on the wireless (or should I say radio, old habits die hard).

I remember one particular night when my father was at work at the Rising Sun Colliery. Bombs had dropped very close to our house and when eventually my father arrived having walked from Wallsend, about 6 miles away, he told us that at the top of the street was a big crater and in the bottom of it was a police box. Those blue police boxes that have now been made obsolete through the mobility of the police cars. He also said a policeman had died. This was at the Quadrant on the Balkwell Estate shown in the photo below. He said that he was almost too scared to come any further in case our house had been hit. Later, he told us that when he had walked home along the Coast Road – which runs parallel to the river about three miles to the north – he could see a display in the sky that reminded him of the front in the First World War. There were searchlights, barrage balloons, flares from enemy planes, flaming onions from the guns, flashes from the shells of the anti-aircraft guns and the flashes from bombs. He said that an eerie green glow covered Tyneside from the incendiary bombs that fell in showers, and fires raged in the huge riverside wood yard of Stephen L. Robson's where pit props were stored, measured and cut for distribution to all the coal pits in the area. This was the same place my mother and I had gone to find prop-ends for firewood.

This is a not very clear photo of the Quadrant where a high explosive bomb landed in the road and a blue police box was lying at the bottom of the huge crater. The damage to surrounding buildings was extensive.

At Maple Crescent a Corporation house (in the Ridges Estate) was demolished by a direct hit and at The Quadrant an HE in the road damaged surrounding property.

This is the school yard of Chirton School. It looks like a shellhole from the First World War. Elsewhere can be seen of the damage to the school and the adjoining church. Thank God there were no children around at the time.

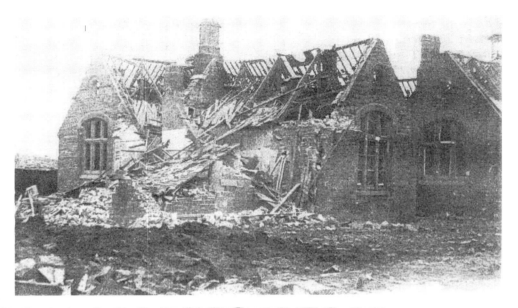

Another view of Chirton School shows the Rex Cinema to the left of the picture. Both were badly damaged and sadly some people died.

Extracts from Monkseaton Secondary School's Log Book

8th April 1941

Air raid involving an alert of 8 hours duration last night resulted in a decline in attendance to 80% as against 90% yesterday. 10% of children thus absent from this cause.

18th April 1941

The week's Fire Watching closes tonight and the following service is gratefully acknowledged, the hours extending over a period of 10 days. Miss Copland 36 hours, Mr Wrangham 30 hours, Miss Craigs 18 hours, Miss Elsdon 15 hours, Miss Stevenson 12 hours, Mr Fawcus (warden) 6 hours. The headmaster was also on watch for periods exceeding 36 hours.

The damage in Oswin Terrace in April 1941. The bomb had landed on the junction of Oswin Terrace and Balkwell Avenue. One person was killed – Mrs Carr.

Billy Mill Lane on 16th April 1941. This damage was caused by the same bombing that hit Chirton School.

No. 6.—Mr F. G. Egner, Town Clerk and Food Executive Officer.

No. 2:
Coun. W. R. Forster,
Chief Warden

No. 11.—Dr R. H. Dawson, Medical Officer of Health.

No. 18.—Mrs A. E. Hill (Tynemouth W.V.S. Organiser).

In 1944 the Shields Evening News published a series of cartoons of the Tynemouth ARP Personalities. Here is a four from over 40 produced. The cartoon of Chief Constable Tom Blackburn on page 35 is also from this series.

Above and below: The aftermath of bombing at Preston Hospital.

An Unforgettable Memory

In 1941, the air raids increased and between April and October of that year there were a number of very heavy raids on North Shields. Two of these, on a Tuesday and Thursday of the same week, were dive-bombing raids by German Stuka aircraft. The terrifying scream of the aircraft, which dived steeply to drop their bombs, would be followed by the shriek of the bomb – with a much shorter life but with terrifying consequences. We used to crouch in the air raid shelter not knowing whether it was our turn next.

During this period I was now delivering newspapers in the early evenings. My paper round started at the east end of the town and ended in the west, which although it consisted only of three long streets, they were in effect all strung together as one long street about 1¹/₂ miles in total length. These were: Trevor Terrace, Queen Alexandra Road and Queen Alexandra Road West. I did not own a bicycle and the delivery took me about two hours. In that time, I could judge after a number of weeks, where I would be when the siren sounded. I was almost always near the end of my round. An air raid shelter was dug into a small pit heap, of the then disused Preston Colliery. This seemed to be an ideal place to wait until the all-clear sounded. At the entrance stood a familiar figure. He was Mr Greenacre, the School Board Man, the terror of the school truants. He was the air raid warden for the area, dressed in his dark blue uniform and tin helmet. He advised me on one occasion to get inside and keep away from the door.

On one such night there was a lull and I decided to make a run for home which was about a mile away. I hared down the road and as I reached the Robin Hood Inn at Chirton, there was an almighty bang as guns fired into the sky. I dashed for shelter and found about six people hiding under a brick arch. I huddled in beside them and you could hear the shrapnel showering down on the road and roofs of nearby houses. During another lull, when we heard the throbbing German planes receding, I dashed out again and finally flung myself headlong into the shelter. My mother had been worried. The following morning I went to the newspaper shop to find a very quiet and mournful group. One of them, a very tall and thin young man called Greenacre had said that his Uncle George Greenacre, Air Raid Warden, had been killed the previous night. His head was blown off outside Preston Colliery air raid shelter. I am glad now that I ran home.

Preston Colliery after its closure.

Some of the people killed in the raid of 1st October 1941

George Greenacre aged 56, Air Raid Warden at Preston Colliery Public Shelter. Decapitation, HE bomb, of 123 Queen Alexander Road West.

Christopher Bailey Cummings aged 67, married, Co-op bakery, Chirton. Firewatcher of 51 Silkey's Lane.

Frederick Pierson aged 42, 15 Saville Street. Clothier of 16 Argyle Street, Tynemouth.

Joan Mary Arnold aged 12, 71 Howdon Road. Daughter of David Arnold.

Dorothy Arnold aged 5 months, 71 Howdon Road. Daughter of David Arnold.

Emma Cooper Henderson aged 34, 71 Howdon Road.

Elizabeth Illey aged 68, 71 Howdon Road.

Ada Arnold aged 34, 71 Howdon Road, of 63 Howdon Road.

Thomas Beams aged 70, 73 Howdon Road.

Jacobus Meyer aged 20, Merchant Seaman. Near Smith's Dock.

Isabella Bell aged 38, married, 40 Elsdon Street.

John Downey Dawson aged 47, 5 Wellington Street. Ship's Rigger.

Margaret Dora Trevis aged 70, Gray's Yard, Nile Street. Home address: 2 Sidney Street.

John Patrick Lydon aged 41, Gray's Yard, Nile Street. Home address: 3 Sidney Street.

George Turnbull aged 73, British Restaurant. Belongs: 27 Dene Street.

Margaret Noble aged 62, 5 Mill Street, Milburn Place.

Mary Ann Steel aged 58, 15 Stanley Street West.

Doreen Steel aged 17, spinster, 15 Stanley Street West.

Georgina Hall aged 29, widow, 23 Victoria Street.

Margaret Ann Hall, 23 Victoria Street.

Marjory Hall aged 1¹/₂, 23 Victoria Street.

Alex McSaley aged 17, 23 Victoria Street.

John Jones Crammon aged 18, 23 Victoria Street.

Martha Ellis aged 67, 25 Victoria Street.

Edith Roberts aged 7, 25 Victoria Street.

Margaret Fraser aged 11, 3A Sidney Street.

Maureen Fraser aged 7, 3A Fraser Street.

Elizabeth Wilson Fraser aged 35, 3A Sidney Street.

Thomas Alexander Turnbull aged 41, Lorry Driver, 19 Morpeth Terrace, Percy Main.

Catherine Turnbull aged 14, 19 Morpeth Terrace, Percy Main.

Catherine Aitken Turnbull aged 44, 19 Morpeth Terrace, Percy Main.

Amy Smith aged 41, 19 Morpeth Terrace. Belongs: 13 Mindrum Terrace, Percy Main.

George Lamb aged 56, near Weslyan Church, Coach Lane. Belongs: 50 Hopper Street.

Mary Ann Henderson aged 48, 31 Scorer Street.

Marjory Henderson aged 17, 31 Scorer Street.

Charles Allison aged 56, 35 Scorer Street.

The devastation left in Heaton Terrace on 5th May 1941. The Docherty family survived the bombing in their Anderson Shelter at No 132. Seven members of the family were rescued from under the rubble.

Queen Victoria School, Coach Lane, after bomb damage in October 1941. The school was badly damaged, five classrooms were found to be unusable, pupils were transferred to the Western Board School. We were told it was an oil bomb and that is proved right. It burned for several days and nights, giving us time to have a look. We also had a look at any other buildings that we had heard had been bombed, while at the same time keeping an eye open for pieces of shrapnel, which we used to swap at school.

Saville Street North Shields. A well known area of the town. Few had not visited Woolworths shown on the left, a popular store before the war. Also, the large hall above used to have vaudeville turns and I remember two, one with performing bull dogs and the other a piper and girl singer. Naturally, my father being a bag piper took us there as kids. I also remember just around the corner of Upper Little Bedford

Street a stall selling fruit. When the father retired the son took over. I forget their name. Perhaps a reader will remember.

A more peaceful view of Saville Street before the War. There are trams, bikes and pedestrians – but no cars.

Devastation of North Shields Gasworks purifying plant Waterville Road. Bombing on Friday 12th & Saturday 13th March 1943. This is one of the pictures not released for publication by the censors at the time.

Bird Street on 2nd October 1941. This bomb killed a policeman behind the blast wall at the corner of Beacon Street. The Robin Hood Inn survived until 1957.

Chapter 5
Wilkinson's Disaster

Had a disaster of this proportion occurred during peacetime, such as a colliery explosion, a factory collapse, or a gasometer blowing up, resulting in so many being killed and injured as at Wilkinson's factory, King Street, it would have hit national headlines and been remembered nationwide for years. However, in the war years with its severe restrictions on news reported, for reasons that we all know, very little was known beyond the boundaries of their own town, except what percolated through via local gossip, but without the stamp of authority. This was the North East's worst single bomb disaster and few outside of North Shields knew about it during the war. My mother thought the shelter had a great atmosphere. She was impressed by the community spirit, saying that everybody joined in with the singing to the tunes from the accordion. She also made reference to a sailor and others in uniform and said she felt safe. I believe she only went to the shelter twice, and what would have been the third time, she decided, along with a neighbour Mrs Sweeting, to go straight home to the kids (us) because the sky was quiet.

Right: An early trade advert for Wilkinson's.

Here is an account of the Wilkinson's disaster from the *North East Diary 1939-1945* website by Roy Ripley and Brian Pears:

Saturday, 3rd/4th May 1941

Tyneside's worst incident of the war occurred when HEs fell on North Shields; one scored a direct hit on Wilkinson's Lemonade Factory at the corner of George Street and King Street, North Shields, where 190 people including many women and children were sheltering in the basement, 105 people died. Whole families were wiped out, including one of six. A soldier was called upon to identify his wife and four children, aged from two to fourteen. One of the heroines of this ghastly night was Mrs Ellen Lee, a woman warden who, although badly burned about the face, rescued thirty-two people from the shelter. Of the other HEs that fell on North Shields, a single HE dropped on George Street, between Church Street and Queen Street. A single HE fell on the railway embankment near to Stephenson Street and a single HE fell at the high water mark on The Flatts. (The Flatts are the Fish Quay Sands). There was major property damage.

Above and right: Two views from after the bomb. A view of Wilkinson's lemonade factory with a basement public air raid Shelter.

Later Painful Memories

In the *News Guardian* of North Tyneside on Thursday 2nd June 1994, a report of that terrible bombing revived painful memories for those who survived and the relations of the deceased. Sixteen survivors met at North Shields Public Library the week prior to the article. One who survived by not going to the shelter as usual was a person called, strangely enough, Ronald Curran (not me) then aged 55 years and now living in Whitley Bay and who lost seven members of his family including his grandmother, aunt, and two of her children, Veronica and Maureen who was buried on the day that it would have been her ninth birthday. He was quoted as saying: "We lived in Sidney

Street at the time and I was only four. I knew there was something wrong. My father had lost his mother. He was dreadfully upset and crying. It was the first time I had seen an adult cry. Until then I thought only children cried. I was told my cannie little grandma had gone. One of our relatives had tried to persuade us to go to a shelter but my mother said, "If we are going to die, We'll die in our own home. We hid in a cupboard".

Author's note: In 1993 when researching my own family in the Local Studies Department of North Shields Central Library, I was passed a copy of this particular Curran family tree with a red asterisk against the seven Curran names of those killed in that air raid shelter.

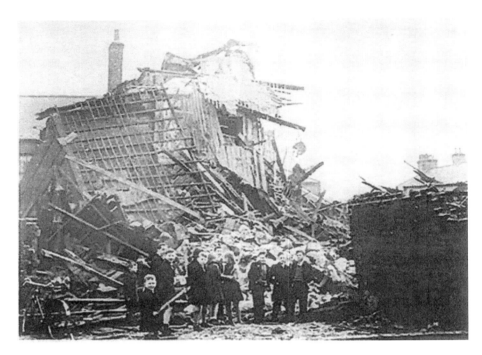

Another photo of the wreckage of Wilkinson's shelter, this time taken of children surveying the damage. Let's hope that none of them had relations among the casualties, but anyone who has seen this as I did shortly after it was hit, will live with the memory all of their life. I went down mainly because my mother and a neighbour, but for an act of Providence, may have been among the victims.

A plaque was unveiled at Beacon Shopping Centre in North Shields as a memorial to those who died during the raid on 3rd May 1941.

This Memorial Plaque was commissioned by the North Tyneside Veterans, North Tyneside Council and North Tyneside Challenge.

In memory of the men, women and children who lost their lives during the air bombing of North Shields on Saturday, 3rd May 1941.

We remember with pride the bravery and dedication of the Emergency and Voluntary Services.

This was the worst bombing incident in the North East of England during World War Two.

Chapter 6
Wartime Memories

Propaganda played an important part in the war effort. Posters such as these helped to promote Government messages as well as boosting morale.

The poster on the right was one of a series featuring the Squanderbug. He was seen as a Nazi agent – complete with Swastikas – encouraging people to waste money and not helping the war effort.

Below are two posters with messages that would not look out of place today. Hoping people will walk rather than take transport would today be seen to help the environment and improve your health. While 'coughs and sneezes spread diseases' is a similar message to the present health authority's swine flu campaign in 2009.

Smith's Dock

I think it is significant that the King and Queen visited North Shields in June 1941, so shortly after the severe bombing of the town and after Wilkinson's shelter disaster in particular. Above: The Queen inspects work at Smith's Dock. Smith's Dock (below) is close to where my wife's Auntie Evelyn lived. It was during the war at this yard that her husband George Sharp fell from a ship's scaffolding into the dock bottom and died several months afterwards.

TELEPHONES NEWCASTLE 26391
NORTH SHIELDS 670

SMITH'S DOCK COMPANY, LIMITED.

SHIPREPAIRERS, SHIPBUILDERS & ENGINEERS.

OFFICES:
REGISTERED OFFICE, NORTH SHIELDS.
SOUTH BANK, MIDDLESBROUGH, YORKS.
31-33, BISHOPSGATE, E.C.2.

TELEGRAPHIC ADDRESSES:
SMITHDOKO, NORTH SHIELDS.
SMITHDOKO, MIDDLESBROUGH.
SMITHDOKO, STOCK, LONDON.

DRY DOCKS:

NORTH SHIELDS.

No. 4	490	FEET.
No. 5	500	FEET.
No. 6	550	FEET.
No. 7	297	FEET.
No. 9	430	FEET (PONTOON)
BAIRDS	160	FEET

MIDDLESBROUGH.

No. 11	575	FEET.
No. 12	400	FEET.
No. 14	550	FEET.
No. 15	450	FEET.

FBI
INCORPORATED BY ROYAL CHARTER

NORTH SHIELDS.

11th October, 1943.

The Garrison Commander,
~~"Avondale",~~ 5, Collingwood Terrace,
~~Rectory Road,~~ Jesmond,
~~Gosforth,~~
Newcastle-on-Tyne.

Dear Sir,

INVASION PRECAUTIONS.

This is to certify that the bearer of this letter - Mr. William Brown, 1, Cromwell Terrace, North Shields, - is one of the two representatives who will contact Military headquarters on our behalf, and in case of emergency, station himself there, in accordance with the arrangements made with the Production Executive, Northern Regional Board.

A photograph of Mr. Brown in Home Guard uniform is attached to this letter, but it is possible that he may be in civilian dress on certain occasions.

Yours faithfully,
FOR SMITH'S DOCK COMPANY, LTD.
R A Stephenson
DIRECTOR & GENERAL MANAGER.

SMITH'S DOCK CO LTD.
11 OCT 1943
NORTH SHIELDS

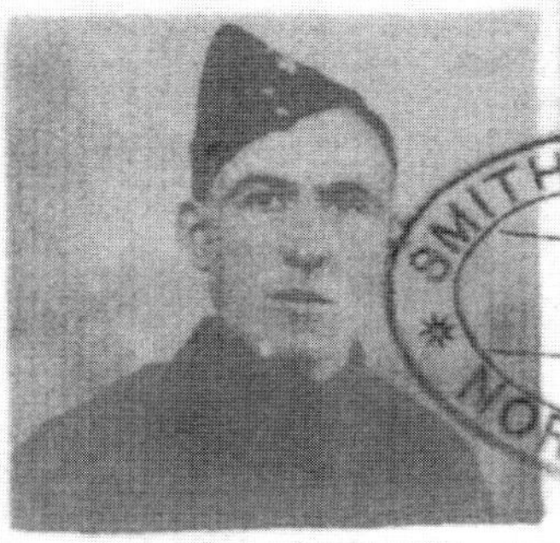

Signed on behalf of
Smith's Docks Home Guard Unit.

H Adarling
Captain. O.C.

Mr. Brown's signature is
appended herewith:

W. Brown

A letter from the Smith's Dock Company informing the Garrison Commander in Newcastle that William Brown (photograph attached) was an appointed representative for the company in case of an invasion.

A Nurse's Story
by Lena Cooper

Lena Cooper was a nurse at Preston Hospital during the war. Here she gives her memories of the hospital:

It was announced by the Prime Minister, Neville Chamberlain, over the radio that Britain and Germany were at war in September 1939. Our whole lives changed because it affected everybody and everything. It was a new way of living and working and, dare I say it, discipline.

At Preston Hospital there was a lot of activity with sandbagging around important parts of the building, entrances etc. All windows during the war had to be covered at night so as not to show any lights in case there were enemy planes about or an air raid was in progress. Everyone was issued and fitted with a gas mask that had to be carried around with you always in case of gas attacks by the enemy.

Some people were helped to make air raid shelters in the middle of their gardens. We had air raid wardens on constant duty because nobody knew just when a raid by the enemy would occur. If there was an air raid warning given then everyone had to get to the shelters as quickly as possible. It was a bit frightening for children and for the elderly. They had to stay there until the 'all-clear' signal was given. Sometimes this meant spending all night in the shelter – not much fun! Eventually, we had a sing-song or some kind of guessing game; anything we could think of to make us forget where we were and why.

It was the same sort of activities at Preston Hospital where I was at the time. Children were taken to shelters accompanied by nurses to look after them. However, a lot of the servicemen patients were unable to be moved so all lighting in the wards was subdued and nurses kept watch. Such relief when the all-clear was sounded. Everyone felt the pressure. When we nurses got a day off it felt in one way a relief for 24 hours but in another feeling it was like 'running away when we should be on duty.'

Nurses and servicemen outside Preston Hospital around 1939. Lena Cooper is far left in the back row. Note the sandbags in the background.

We had air raid wardens at home and they had to ensure that no lights of any kind were visible from outside our homes or any building that was in use at the time. Even when an air raid was over and we got the 'all-clear' signal the blackout situation remained. Our only consolation, if there was one, was that we knew that the whole country was also having to put up with these conditions and usually facing greater danger than we were.

Rationing of food started as early as four months after the declaration of war, with bacon, butter and sugar being the first goods on ration. Meat was rationed in March then tea, cooking fats and margarine in about July. Most other foods were gradually added to rationing. It was a difficult job trying to make your rations last. Of course we were issued with ration books and we had to use these coupons when buying our allotted ration of any foods. I think the food rationing went on until 1954 and I'm pretty sure that I still have in my 'archives' my old ration book. We were also all given books of clothing coupons.

The food rationing was at first very difficult to live with but on reflection it was probably better for us health-wise. We could not even imagine how dried egg powder could ever replace a fresh egg but like everything we got used to it. Dried egg was best used in baking or puddings and then it was more acceptable but only just!

The government of the day launched a 'Dig for Victory' campaign and people were encouraged to dig up their flowerbeds and grow vegetables. People living in the country were better off for this purpose because they had more space and also access to berries, mushrooms and other wild foods that town-dwellers did not have.

As a result of this campaign we were able to have fresh vegetables grown in our own gardens and this was very acceptable to us country folk. We all had to survive and keep healthy as best we could. Even people at home had to make some contribution to the war-effort.

I have to admit I was never able to accept dried egg powder for any meal that I prepared so I usually avoided recipes in which it was required. I think the equivalent to one fresh egg was one level tablespoon of egg powder plus two level tablespoons of water. I think they had to be mixed together and then stand for five minutes until the powder had absorbed all the moisture then beaten with a fork, removing any lumps.

The egg powder could be added dry to a recipe for plain cakes or puddings, mixing with the other dry ingredients but, when liquid was added to the mixture, two tablespoons extra per dry egg had to be allowed. Funnily, I could cope with everything else in the rationing scheme of things but not dried egg powder.

Fortunately, there were much more serious things to cope with than this so it was soon relegated to the bottom of my 'action list.' Little did we know how long the war would go on. Some people reckoned it would be over by Christmas. We could not have envisaged that it would be well into 1945 before peace was declared.

Lena Cooper at the end of the War.

The 'Really Cold' War
by Ron Curran

I have good reason to remember the winters of 1941 and 1942 for as long as I live. In 1941 I was an errand boy for a bloke called Mr Llewellyan who had a small general grocer shop in Nile Street, North Shields. I think it would be either January or February 1941 and the snow had been falling for two days continuously, and he asked me to deliver some groceries including eggs to a house in Cullercoats on my bicycle. I couldn't believe my ears. The snow was belting down and although the roads had been gritted they were far from clear. Cullercoats was about two and half miles towards the coast and, because he was the boss, I got on my bike and went. I hadn't travelled several hundred yards before I had to get off my bike and push. I did this until I was tired, pushing through about five inches of snow. When I reached Northumberland Park near the Golf Course, I decided to get back on the bike. However, anybody who knows this road knows that there is a hill up towards the Dolphin Pub and the bike skidded and the goods rolled out the basket. It was inevitable that the eggs would be broken. I remember crying when I reached the house and the lady was very sympathetic with me and said she could have waited until the roads were clear. When I arrived back in the town the shop was shut so I went home, at least an hour late. Cutting a long story short, my mother was blistering about Mr Lewelyan and said she was going to see him the following day, which she did. It ended up that I left the job and started at Wakefield's Garage as an odd job boy. That was the most memorable winter's day of 1941.

In 1942, on the day that the snow started to fall, the sky turned black and some of the largest snowflakes I have ever seen fell steadily throughout the day. In the evening, a neighbour called Mr Liddle knocked at the door and asked my mother if we (the boys) were in and, if so, could he have a word with us about the snow. My dad was at work but due home anytime. Mr Liddle was an air raid warden and wearing his tin hat and arm band. He asked my brother Ian and I if we would help to clear the snow in the

Westgate Road, Newcastle during the winter of 1941.

morning 'to keep the traffic moving'. We were delighted to be asked. I was going on fourteen and Ian was a year older than me. The following morning we opened the front door and to our delight, and astonishment, we found the snow level with the top of the three steps to our house from the path. We couldn't wait to get shovels out from under the stairs and start to clear our steps and so, slowly but surely, to the front street. That took about two hours. After a spell and some hot drinks, we were back again in the street and saw to our amazement, telegraph wires sagging under the weight of about six inches of snow. I never for one moment thought that it was possible for snow to stick to wire so much so that the poles were lying towards each other. The silence was deafening. We must have thought the same thing simultaneously. Nobody else was in sight, including the air raid warden. The street was eerily silent. It was a white wilderness in a council estate. The snow was the deepest in my memory up to that time and even the terrible snow storms of 1947 cannot surpass 1942 as the heaviest snowfall. There was snow in the shaded part of people's gardens up to the last week of May. We returned to the house in disgust, as much because we couldn't chuck snowballs at anybody but ourselves, as the fact that nobody else was helping.

When I was discussing these winters with a friend in the local pub in Belford where I now live, he said: "Wait a minute." He popped over the road where he lived and on returning passed to me a number of photographs of the snowfall of 1942 in Belford – one of which I print here.

Belford, the village where we live now, under snow in 1942.

Wartime Memorabilia

Above: An Air Raid Precautions card for the County of Northumberland – covering North Shields and the surrounding area.

Above: A National Registration Identity Card. The instructions on the back of the card says: 'Always carry your Identity Card. You must produce it on demand by a Police Officer in uniform or member of HM Armed Forces in uniform on duty.'

Right: A page from a leaflet issued by the Ministry of Information giving instructions to the public: 'If the Invader Comes – What to do and how to do it.'

Issued by the Ministry of Information in co-operation with the War Office and the Ministry of Home Security.

If the INVADER comes

WHAT TO DO — AND HOW TO DO IT

THE Germans threaten to invade Great Britain. If they do so they will be driven out by our Navy, our Army and our Air Force. Yet the ordinary men and women of the civilian population will also have their part to play. Hitler's invasions of Poland, Holland and Belgium were greatly helped by the fact that the civilian population was taken by surprise. They did not know what to do when the moment came. *You must not be taken by surprise.* This leaflet tells you what general line you should take. More detailed instructions will be given you when the danger comes nearer. Meanwhile, read these instructions carefully and be prepared to carry them out.

I

When Holland and Belgium were invaded, the civilian population fled from their homes. They crowded on the roads, in cars, in carts, on bicycles and on foot, and so helped the enemy by preventing their own armies from advancing against the invaders. You must not allow that to happen here. Your first rule, therefore, is :—

(1) IF THE GERMANS COME, BY PARACHUTE, AEROPLANE OR SHIP, YOU MUST REMAIN WHERE YOU ARE. THE ORDER IS " STAY PUT ".

If the Commander in Chief decides that the place where you live must be evacuated, he will tell you when and how to leave. Until you receive such orders you must remain where you are. If you run away, you will be exposed to far greater danger because you will be machine-gunned from the air as were civilians in Holland and Belgium, and you will also block the roads by which our own armies will advance to turn the Germans out.

II

There is another method which the Germans adopt in their invasion. They make use of the civilian population in order to create confusion and panic. They spread false rumours and issue false instructions. In order to prevent this, you should obey the second rule, which is as follows :—

(2) DO NOT BELIEVE RUMOURS AND DO NOT SPREAD THEM. WHEN YOU RECEIVE AN ORDER, MAKE QUITE SURE THAT IT IS A TRUE ORDER AND NOT A FAKED ORDER. MOST OF YOU KNOW YOUR POLICEMEN AND YOUR A.R.P. WARDENS BY SIGHT, YOU CAN TRUST THEM. IF YOU KEEP YOUR HEADS, YOU CAN ALSO TELL WHETHER A MILITARY OFFICER IS REALLY BRITISH OR ONLY PRETENDING TO BE SO. IF IN DOUBT ASK THE POLICE-MAN OR THE A.R.P. WARDEN. USE YOUR COMMON SENSE.

Mr. S. Tait. Mr. J. Waterworth.	Mar 22	Apl 3	Apl 15	Apl 27	May 9	May 21	Jun 2	Jun 14	Jun 26	Jul 8	Jul 20
Mr. A. Stapley. Mr. A. Tait.	23	4	16	28	10	22	3	15	27	9	21
Mr. J. Foster. Mr. T. Corcoran.	24	5	17	29	11	23	4	16	28	10	22
Mrs. Dagg. Mr. E. Roberts.	25	6	18	30	12	24	5	17	29	11	23
Mr. Henderson. Miss Henderson.	26	7	19	May 1	13	25	6	18	30	12	24
Mr. Osborne. Mr. Barrow.	27	8	20	2	14	26	7	19	Jul 1	13	25
Mr. Couchman. Mrs. Couchman.	28	9	21	3	15	27	8	20	2	14	26
Mr. J. Dugdale. Mr. W. Dugdale.	29	10	22	4	16	28	9	21	3	15	27
Mr. W. Brown, Jnr. Mr. Stapylton.	30	11	23	5	17	29	10	22	4	16	28
Mr. T. Purvis. Mr. F. Purvis.	31	12	24	6	18	30	11	23	5	17	29
Mr. P. J. Athey. Mrs. Potts.	Apl 1	13	25	7	19	31	12	24	6	18	30
Mr. S. Armstrong. Miss Armstrong.	2	14	26	8	20	Jun 1	13	25	7	19	31

ANYONE NOT ABLE TO TAKE ROSTERED TURN MUST PROVIDE A SUBSTITUTE.

The firewatching roster for two streets in North Shields – Percy Crescent and Cockburn Terrace – from March to July 1943. Firewatching was compulsory and those on watch had to report any damage caused by incendiary bombs. The roster says: 'Anyone not able to take rostered turn must provide a substitute'.

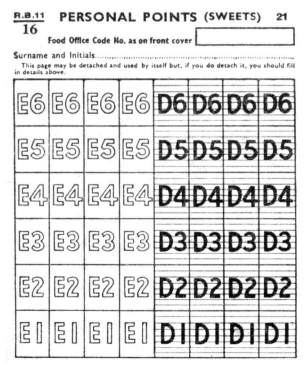

The points page for sweets – every child's favourite page in the ration book.

The front cover of the Souvenir Programme for Newcastle's Victory Celebrations in 1946.

'Why, Joe—not finished yet?'

When you suddenly find you've mastered the job you've been learning, and can pay back some of the friendly teasing that went with your tuition—what fun it can be, on a farm! In an office, it isn't quite the same. 'Still typing that letter, Sheila?' wouldn't get much of a laugh . . . It's the difference of working as one of a small, skilled farm team whose members know each other and help each other: where the boss of the farm is one of the team too. One of those little differences that, for the right woman, can help to make life on the land the happiest job of all.

JOIN THE WOMEN'S LAND ARMY

Post this **COUPON** for further information	To Womens Land Army, Dept. 15H , 6, Chesham St., London, SW1. Send details, please
	NAME..
	ADDRESS..
	.... (Use Id. Stamp—unsealed envelope)

Issued by the Ministry of Labour and National Service in conjunction with the Ministry of Agriculture

Left: An advert for the Women's Land Army. With a shortage in the male workforce during the war, women were recruited to take their place. The Women's Land Army worked on farms providing vital food supplies.

Below: The Blackout was a dangerous environment and this poster advises people to count to 15 slowly before stepping out into the dark – giving your eyes time to adjust.

Left: A poster encouraging people to eat home grown potatoes rather than bread made with wheat that needed to be imported.

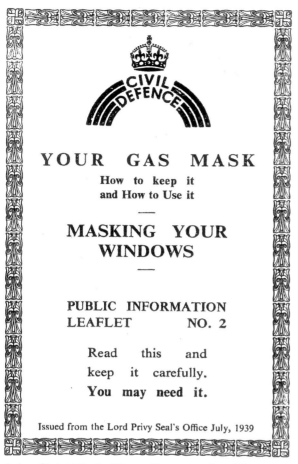

A leaflet titled: *Your Gas mask – How to Keep it and How to Use it.*

A leaflet titled 'Anti-Gas Protection of Babies and Young Children.'

MINISTRY OF HOME SECURITY

ANTI-GAS PROTECTION
OF BABIES AND
YOUNG CHILDREN

Crown Copyright Reserved

LONDON : HIS MAJESTY'S STATIONERY OFFICE : 1939

CONTENTS

	Page
GENERAL MEMORANDUM	I
Description of the Small Child's Respirator ..	I
Description of the Baby's Protective Helmet ..	3
The Choice of the right Protective Device ..	4
INSTRUCTIONS FOR USE OF BABY'S PROTECTIVE HELMET	6
INSTRUCTIONS FOR USE OF SMALL CHILD'S RESPIRATOR	7

July, 1939

(393.) 32736. Wt. 29376-641. 500M. 9/41. A., P. & S., Ltd. 428.

OFFICIAL INSTRUCTIONS ISSUED BY THE MINISTRY OF HOME SECURITY

GAS ATTACK

HOW TO PUT ON YOUR GAS MASK

Always keep your gas mask with you – day and night. Learn to put it on quickly. Practise wearing it.

1. Hold your breath. 2. Hold mask in front of face, with thumbs inside straps.
3. Thrust chin well forward into mask, pull straps over head as far as they will go.
4. Run finger round face-piece taking care head-straps are not twisted.

Official instructions on how to put on your gas mask. There was a great fear at the beginning of the war that the Germans would use gas. However, unlike the First World War, gas was never used.

The *Whitley Seaside Chronicle* printed details of air raid shelters in the area.

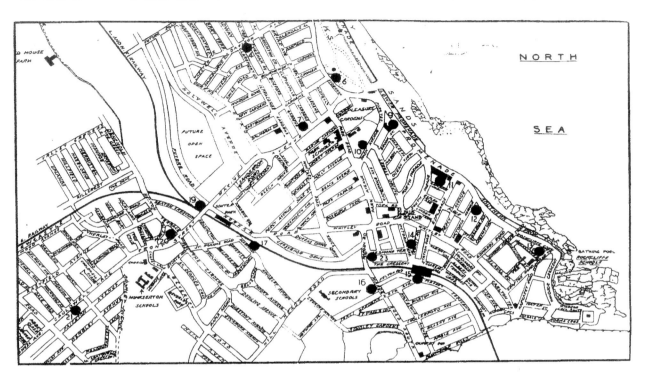

Public Shelters

No	Address	Accommodation
4	Junction of Davison Avenue and Claremont Road, Monkseaton	100
6	Junction of Promenade and Marine Avenue	100
7	Marine Avenue, junction with Cliftonville Gardens	200
9	Opposite Avenue Hotel, Promenade	100
10	Whitley Park	300
11	Tennis Courts behind Rex Hotel, Promenade	100
12	Tennis Court, junction of Helena Avenue with Promenade	200
13	Tennis Court, junction of Grafton Road with Promenade	200
14	Junction of Victoria Terrace and Trewitt Road	150
15	Plessey Crescent	100
16	Whitley & Monkseaton School Playing Field, Marden Rd	50
17	Marmion Terrace Recreation Ground	100
19	Junction of Hartley Avenue and Marine Avenue	100
20	Adjoining Monkseaton Arms, Front Street	100
21	Cauldwell Lane opposite junction with Holmwood Avenue	100
23	Crescent Vale, opposite Provincial Laundry	200

Holidays at Home
by Norman Christenson

Men in bowler hats in far off London seemed always to be preoccupied with 'keeping up moral' even though ours never seemed to be all that down. One of their greatest schemes was the 'Holidays at Home' programme which somebody in our far-off capital decided would be a great fillip for folks who couldn't travel to Cannes or the Riviera this year. It was a real bonus for the likes of us who hadn't even realised that you could go anywhere further than Tynemouth or Whitley Bay for the day so we descended, with every other urchin from miles around, on the big Marquee the troupe had erected in Smith's Park. Sat on hard benches under this great canopy, we scrunched up closer and closer till just about every resident from the upper and lower Ridges had piled in. You could tell the lower Ridges ones because they were the ones who wore their jumpers back to front and looked dead poor. Eventually a man with a fair isle jumper (on the right way) and baggy pants jumped on the stage and asked "Is everybody HAPPY" and nobody said no and then he told these fantastic jokes like when is a door not a door, before another man in a fair isle jumper started pounding away on this piano as we all roared our way through the mandatory sing song. Then more excitement as kids went in the balloon blowing up race, then a skipping competition and a game where they spilled water they were supposed to be balancing on their heads and didn't even get hit by their Ma.

This frenzy of excitement and entertainment climaxed when the first fair isle man called for volunteers to sing something for the relaxed and appreciative audience. At this,

A poster showing what was on for 'Holidays at Home'.

everybody sat and looked at everybody else, wondering who would be brave or foolhardy enough to get up in front of this huge crowd. The embarrassed silence was broken by a few tentative claps which soon built to resounding roar of applause as the audience spotted the urchin-like figure of none other than cousin John McDonald, walking towards the stage. Dressed in sagging socks, scuffed shoes, a tattered jumper and sporting that terrible Ridges haircut of a fringe in front and bald everywhere else. He confidently whispered his selection to the fair isle jumper at the piano while the Master of Ceremonies waited to give him the big intro. Our little family group sat and looked at each other in stunned disbelief as it was common knowledge John was absolutely and irreversibly tone deaf. Undeterred by this minor disability, he plunged into a rendition of *The White Cliffs of Dover* the likes of which had never been heard before or since. The pianist tried every key except the one to their Bedford truck, the audience squirmed, the MC tried to put on his 'Isn't he a brave little chap' face and we tried to look as if we'd never seen him before. It's not generally known that the observation that 'War is Hell' was first expressed at this recital.

Chapter 7
Counting The Cost

County Boroughs	Killed	Injured and Detained in Hospital	Slightly Injured
Sunderland	273	389	725
Tynemouth	220	163	274
South Shields	152	294	287
Newcastle	141	178	409
Middlesbrough	88	158	421
West Hartlepool	46	50	84
Darlington	—	2	8
Gateshead	5	1	12
Totals	**925**	**1,235**	**2,220**

Total killed or injured – 4,380

About fifty German Bombers raided South Shields on 2nd October 1941. Twelve people were killed. The photograph shows the Market Place after the raid.

The Winter Gardens in Mowbray Park, Sunderland were badly damaged in a raid in April 1941. It was not until the end of the century that the Winter Gardens were re-built.

Northumberland County

	Killed	Injured and Detained in Hospital	Slightly Injured
Alnwick RDC	10	16	42
Castle Ward RDC	1	-	-
Norham & Islandshire RDC	-	-	34
Rothbury RDC	-	3	-
Amble UDC	-	-	2
Ashington UDC	1	19	44
Bedlington UDC	-	2	18
Longbenton UDC	6	10	21
Newbiggin UDC	7	5	3
Newburn UDC	3	-	20
Seaton Valley UDC	6	11	23
Whitley Bay/Monkseaton UDC	34	43	184
Berwick MB	21	4	51
Blyth MB	4	12	146
Wallsend MB	36	34	88
Totals	**129**	**159**	**676**

Total killed or injured – 964

This busy scene on the Tyne shows why the river was such an important target for German bombers.

It would be un-generous of me to make no reference to Hull, a northern seaport town which suffered a blitz comparable in devastation to many other blitzed cities in Britain, with the exception of London. This may be disputed, but after all, Hull is only a small city. Hull had 815 alerts and spent over 1,000 hours under alerts. 1,200 people were killed; 3,000 were injured and received treatment. 152,000 people were rendered temporarily homeless and provided for. 250 domestic shelters and 120 communal shelters were destroyed, from which more than 800

Women workers take a break in a North East shipyard during the Second World War.

people were rescued alive. By the end of hostilities, approximately 6,000 of the 93,000 homes in Hull had escaped bomb damage, from the three main attacks in March and May 1941 plus many smaller raids favoured by the Germans for the easy approach across the North Sea. Altogether Hull weathered 70 large and small night attacks from piloted aircraft compared with Southampton (49), Bristol (51), and London (251) plus 101 by day. A study by a group of Hull citizens reported that 26 reception centres dealt with 1,773 admissions after the first but smaller raid in March 1941. By the evening of the 16th March 1941, two days before the much larger blitz, 3,294 persons were seeking help of some sort, 2,216 of them for rehousing. The very heavy raid of 18th March 1941 when nearly 400 bombers in an aerial bombardment lasting from 21.15 to 04.00 the following morning, stepped up the pressure on the reception centres even more. The 7th/8th May double raid shook the populace once again and raids across the North Sea continued into July 1941 when the rest of the country was practically at peace again. An observer in autumn of 1941 described Hull as 'the only town to have been heavily raided since the German attack on Russia'. In September 1939, Hull had 92,660 houses of varying sizes and values, but all capable of accommodating families. In the course of the war: 1,472 were totally destroyed, 2,882 so badly damaged that demolition may be necessary, 3,789 needed repairs beyond the scope of first aid, 11,589 were seriously damaged but patched up, 66,983 were slightly damaged – a total of 86,715. These figures show that only 5,945 houses escaped damage in any form. Some of the 86,715 were struck more than once, in some instances twice and thrice, so that altogether 146,915 houses were damaged.

This photograph was taken in 1944, one year before the war in Europe came to a close. It is a Fancy Dress Parade at Ralph Gardner School (my own school) and my wife Doreen, at the age of 14 years, can be seen as Mrs Mop, holding the mop in her left hand, to the right of the picture. Her sister Lilian, 12 years, is shown (sitting) just right of centre with a chef's hat on her head. It is a signal that life goes on despite the trials and tribulations of war.

By 1945, a number of events in the field of war was rapidly bringing the war to a close. In Europe it was the storming of Berlin by the allied troops – the Russians in the East and the Americans, British and their allies in the West, rushing to get there first. And the ultimate result of that was the building of the Berlin Wall by the Russians, and the establishing of an East Berlin and East Germany under Russian domination. It was about forty years later that I would visit East Berlin only a few years before the tearing down of the Berlin Wall. But the fall of Berlin marked the end of German domination of Europe.

In the Far East it was the dropping of the atom bombs on Hiroshima and Nagasaki, and the quick capitulation of the Japanese. We therefore had VE Day (Victory in Europe) 8th May 1945 and VJ Day (Victory over Japan) on 14th August 1945. I remember waiting for the lights going on to celebrate the end of the blackout. However, we had to wait for the darker night which were still several months away. If one was to encapsulate in three words the feeling of the nation, I would say it was a gasp of relief.

This is a short resume for what seemed a very long war. North Shields is not a small place and it seemed to get more than its fair share of attention from the German bombers. I believed I knew personally about where almost every bomb was dropped on the town. It became a great interest for kids to see what had happened to their town, but I was a paper boy for about a year and it wasn't difficult to see how much damage had occurred from the raids. So much so that I wrote this book for posterity, to let people know 'we took a hell of a hammering'.

Chapter 8
Victory in Europe

When the war in Europe ended in 1945, it seemed as though a spring was released among the population. Tensions that had been suppressed, born of fear of death or mutilation through bombing, and or in many cases fear that their loved ones in the forces may not return. Or even that their houses may be destroyed or damaged. Other tensions caused by rationing, blackout and limited travel were swept aside on the day the war ended. Although not appreciated at the time and even now perhaps not fully understood, the mood of the people had changed. A general election was held and Labour swept to power with an overwhelming majority in the House of Commons, and the biggest surprise of all, if not shock, was the removal from office of the country's wartime leader Winston Churchill as Prime Minister. He was the rock upon which the nation stood and depended upon his leadership to win us through the ravages of war. Now it looked as if an ungrateful nation had tossed him aside as a disposable asset whose purpose had been served and just said – 'thank you very much'! It was however, a mood that swept the country for change after a devastating war.

Winston Churchill visiting a Tyneside shipyard during the First World War.

However, whatever the political consequences this did not stop the jubilation of the citizens all over Britain celebrating on the streets in street parties, dances or merely looking out of their windows beaming at everybody that passed. North Shields was no exception.

Mrs Churchill also played her part in boosting the moral of the British people. Here she is visiting a North East shipyard and giving a wave to some of the workers.

74

Daily Mirror

Tuesday, May 8, 1945
No. 12,911   ONE PENNY
Registered at G.P.O. as a Newspaper.

THIS IS VE-DAY
TODAY, TOMORROW NATIONAL HOLIDAY

And this was London waiting for the VE news

This picture was taken in Piccadilly at five o'clock last evening, two and a half hours after the Germans had broadcast to the world that they had accepted unconditional surrender and that the war in Europe was over after five years, eight months and four days.

The front page of the Daily Mirror celebrates Victory in Europe.

I show right an impromptu get together of neighbours and children following a street party of Hazelwood Avenue North Shields which includes my wife, then Doreen Stoneman, 15 years, her two sisters and brother who are respectively Lilian Stoneman, 13 years, Annette Stoneman, 5 years, and Grenville Stoneman, 10 years. Doreen is two to the right of the lamp post second back row, Lilian, smaller (and very blond) again in second back row, Grenville next to her and one below him (blond) wavy haired Annette.

We consider we are very lucky to have this family photograph. By this time their mother had died the year before and their father who was in Air Sea Rescue was somewhere in the north of Scotland. Doreen was now the housekeeper at an early age, and still smiling.

Waterville Road Street Party. This street is just behind Hazelwood Avenue and where a house, demolished by a bomb, is just off the photo to the right. The old dear to the extreme right next to the tree is dressed all in black, perhaps someone she lost in the bombing?

A happy street party in Laet Street almost overlooking Borough (Bank) Road, the steep bank down to the Ferry Landing, the bottom of the street overlooking the River Tyne.

This area was badly bombed and not surprisingly there are some rather sombre faces. Mind, I think it was before they had their celebration tea, looking at the table. Doreen's Aunty Evelyn lived around the corner at the bottom of Coach Lane very near the Smith's Dock.

"Here you are—don't lose it again"

Right: A cartoon from the Daily Mirror on VE Day.

Acknowledgements

The author would like to thank:

North Tyneside Libraries, North Shields, especially Local Studies Department staff for their willing assistance at all times. The Libraries Department were most helpful in advising and assisting me at the book's draft stage and allowing me to reproduce photographs of bomb damage of North Shields. Also for the copy of the Curran family killed at Wilkinson's Air Raid Shelter.

To Mr Brian Pears for allowing me to reproduce data relating to bombing raids in North Shields in the invaluable *North East Diary 1939-1945* – Roy Ripley & Brian Pears. Copyright Brian Pears 1994-2009. www.ne-diary.bpears.org.uk

To my wife Doreen for providing me with family photographs of their street party and school play during wartime. Also her memory of a tragic evacuation of the family and relations to Rennington near Alnwick.

To Andrew Clark of Summerhill Books for his support and advice, for which I am very grateful.

The publishers would also like to thank the following for photographs and information:

Geoffrey Berriman, Kevin Brady, Alan Brett, Lena Cooper, Philip Curtis, Vera Hook, George Nairn and Sharyn Taylor.

Two more wartime posters. On the left the Squanderbug is again used to highlight waste while on the right the Women's Voluntary Services are promoted.

Happier times in North Shields with a crowd at New Quay.

Bibliography

Around Meadow Well by Pat Hope (2000)

Chirton & Percy Main by Pat Hope (2001)

County Durham & Northumberland During The Second World War by Geoffrey Berriman (2005)

Glimpses of Old North Shields by Andrew Clark & George Nairn (2008)

The Most Dangerous Enemy – A History of the Battle of Britain by Stephen Bungay (2001)

North Shields – Plodgin Through The Clarts by Norman Christenson (1999)

North East Boxing Book by Alan Brett & Bill Wood (1995)

Sunderland Blitz by Kevin Brady (1999)

Sunderland Shipyards by Andrew Clark (1998)

Thanks for the Memories by Lena Cooper (2008)

Tyneside at War by Clive Hardy & Paul Harris (1988)

Wallsend Shipyards by Andrew Clark & Wallsend People's Centre (1999)

Women of Old County Durham by Margaret McReady (2002)

Daily Express
Daily Mirror
Evening Chronicle
Evening News
Morning News
News Guardian
Sunderland Echo
Whitley Seaside Chronicle

Also available from Summerhill Books

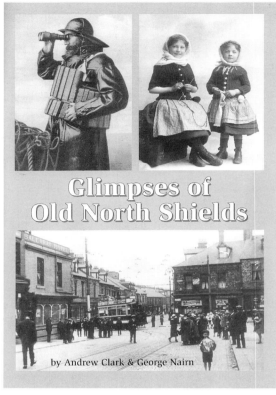

**Glimpses of
Old North Shields**

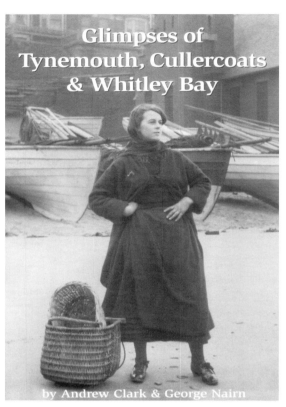

**Glimpses of Tynemouth,
Cullercoats & Whitley Bay**

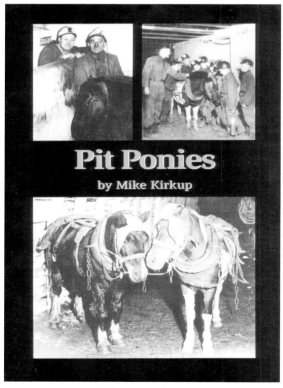

Pit Ponies
The story of pit ponies in the
Northumberland & Durham Coalfields

Wallsend Best
A Personal Experience of the
Rising Sun Colliery